just one more thing

just one

PETER FALK

more thing

Carroll & Graf Publishers ■ New York

JUST ONE MORE THING
Stories from My Life

Carroll & Graf Publishers
An Imprint of Avalon Publishing Group, Inc.
245 West 17th Street, 11th Floor
New York, NY 10011

AVALON
publishing group incorporated

First Carroll & Graf edition 2006
First paperback edition 2007

Library of Congress Cataloging-in-Publication Data is available.

ISBN-13: 978-0-78671-939-6
ISBN-10: 0-7867-1939-7

9 8 7 6 5 4 3 2 1

Interior design by Pauline Neuwirth

Printed in the United States of America
Distributed by Publishers Group West

To my lovely wife,
the light of my life,
and all the dogs

contents

foreward   xv

on being nominated for an academy award   1

you have you stories and i have eye stories   5

my wife shera   10

thinking about faye dunaway while driving   13

on being a young man who has no idea what
he wants to do with his life
(p.s. and he is in no hurry to find out)   17

i graduate college—next day paris   23

on working to get a master's degree in a field
you have no interest in and no aptitude for   29

on the thin line dividing naïveté from stupidity,
or why it took 12 years to become an actor   35

on the four words that broke the camel's back   39

the big apple and my first play   41

the iceman cometh   **43**

jason robards tells a good story   **47**

on being an actor with one eye   **49**

marjorie morningstar   **53**

leo penn's ad-lib   **57**

on my wedding day   **59**

my father   **63**

i have never been arrested in the united states
but i have been arrested in . . .   **71**

murder, inc.   **75**

on my first meeting with frank capra   **81**

on wanting to kiss frank capra   **83**

on the role overcoats can play in an actor's career   **87**

making a movie in russia—why?!   **91**

it's a mad, mad, mad, mad world   **97**

robin and the seven hoods   **101**

the great race   **107**

arthur miller tells a good story   **111**

on what i had and you didn't—a lou lilly in my life   113

getting arrested in genoa   121

the raisin story   127

anzio   129

how did the columbo character evolve?   135

columbo odds and ends—to play columbo—
makeup not required—unlike some other actors   143

"this old man, he played one—
he played knickknack on my thumb"   145

columbo odds and ends—god never designed
any one human to be recognized by two billion other humans   149

columbo odds and ends—descriptions   151

what's the toughest thing about creating a columbo?   153

great clues   159

the early days—the fights—the disputes—the distrust   165

in summit meetings called to settle disputes,
where the star of a tv series sits can be decisive   167

peter falk's ad-lib   171

shera stories   175

john cassavetes   181

first meeting with john   185

husbands   189

a woman under the influence   193

what is a cassavetes set like?   195

getting a laugh   197

cassavetes—a tribute   201

neil simon   203

actors as artists   211

drawing art students' league   213

a message to the people of romania   221

can movie directors help movie actors? if so, how?   225

on why i wasn't in *the godfather*   231

why marlon brando wears an earplug   233

the brink's job   237

the in-laws   243

how *the in-laws* began   247

the in-laws: years later, alan and i share a joyous moment   251

contents

wings of desire   **257**

the princess bride   **263**

happy new year   **267**

roommates   **273**

epilogue   **281**

contents   xiii

foreward

WHEN I WAS growing up, a biography was the life of Abe Lincoln. Today every fifth person is a legend or icon. I go into Nate and Al's, a delicatessen in Beverly Hills, and in the next booth there are three icons sitting there eating pastrami sandwiches.

so this is not an autobiography!

To be honest, I don't know what you'd call it. I know it's funny—you'll laugh a lot. And when I talk about Columbo, it's interesting. He absorbed me—

and how he evolved will absorb you.

There's a chapter on Marlon Brando. He never acted without wearing a plug in his ear. That's a fact and all of us actors were fascinated. When you read about it, I believe you will be as consumed as I was.

i also like to draw. picasso i'm not.

But it's a big part of my life.

My idea of heaven is to wake up, have a good breakfast, and spend the rest of the day drawing, but this book is not about drawing. You'll decide what it's about. My object is to keep you awake.

WHAT MICHELANGELO SAID TO THE POPE

Upon seeing the completed Sistine Chapel the Pope congratulated Michelangelo on his work. Michelangelo replied, "It's all in the drawing. The rest I can get by pissing on it."

WHAT'S WRITTEN ON DEGAS'S TOMBSTONE

"Here lies a fellow who liked to draw"

While we're on Degas: When asked how he felt when a painting of his sold for a record breaking one million francs he said, "I feel like the horse that won the Kentucky Derby and they fed him the same old bag of oats."

ENOUGH ABOUT THESE TWO FELLAS

let's get on to my stuff!

Young Dancer

Woman with Bowler Hat

enough of my stuff!

let's start the book.

just one more thing

on being nominated for an academy award

IT WAS 1955. I was 28 and I had decided to become an actor. I told my father and he said, "You gonna paint your face and make an ass of yourself the rest of your life?" I said, "That's right." He shook my hand and said good luck.

I quit my job. I was working for the Budget Director of the State of Connecticut as an efficiency expert (the truth is the first day on the job I couldn't find the office—it was in the state capitol—I ended up in the post office). Anyway, I gave up posing as an efficiency expert, announced to the world I was an actor, and moved to New York City, Greenwich Village—the heart of the off-Broadway theater. For the next four years I kicked around off-Broadway doing plays, $10.00 a week rehearsal, $30.00 a week when the show opened.

In 1960, Hollywood—more precisely Twentieth Century Fox—came to New York to make the film *Murder, Inc.* They brought the two stars and hired local New York actors to play the mobsters. I got the part of the lead hood, Abe "Kid Twist" Reles. This was a big deal—a very big deal—my first Hollywood movie.

The picture came out, I got splashy reviews. It was a gloomy, gray afternoon in the bowels of a Greenwich Village saloon where I was sitting with Sal Mineo and Ben Gazzara. The newspaper reviews were on the table in front of us. Sal said, "You should campaign for an Academy Award." Campaign!!! What's that? It didn't sound right. You campaign when you run for mayor but actors don't campaign. Sal said they did. They take out ads. Ads! Where? "The Hollywood trade papers," Sal said. Another thing I never heard of. Sal said it happens. He had been a kid actor in Hollywood so I believed him but it seemed ridiculously farfetched. Hollywood, movie stars, Academy Awards, gorgeous women, that's another world. Sal was just being nice but I couldn't take it seriously.

That same year, I got a gig on *The Untouchables*—a TV show shot in Los Angeles. My first trip to HOLLYWOOD. At the motel there was a message from my agent. His boss, Abe Lastfogel, the legendary head of William Morris, the world's biggest talent agency, wanted to see me. Why me? I couldn't imagine.

Mr. Lastfogel didn't waste any time. After a nice greeting he said, "You should campaign for an Academy Award."

"That's what Sal Mineo said."

"Well, do it!"

"What do I do?"

"Take out ads, hire a press agent—spend money!"

That's what I did, and what do you know—I got nominated.

Now it's the big night. The Academy Awards. The press agent and I are in our seats. We get to my category and I hear a voice say, "And the winner is Peter . . ." I'm rising out of my seat ". . . Ustinov." I'm heading back down. When I hit the seat I turned to the press agent and say, "You're fired." I didn't want him charging me for another day.

---

* Ustinov won for his performance in *Spartacus*.

you have
you stories
and i have
eye stories

WHEN I WAS three years old my preschool teacher called my mother and said she wondered if there was something wrong with my eyes. Many times during the day I would cock my head in this unnatural way in order to look at something. She wondered right. The doctor told my mother I had cancer of the eye and it had to be removed and yesterday was not too soon.

My mother, God love her, moved fast. She took me to two more doctors that same day, and they all said the same thing: it was a cancerous tumor, a well-known eye cancer, retina blastoma, and it could kill. I was operated on two days later. Probably the earliest memory of my life was in the hospital on the morning of the operation standing in front of the elevator with my mother. When the elevator arrived my mother said, "Oh my goodness, I forgot my pocketbook" and then she told me to get in the elevator and tell the doctors to wait, she'd be right back. I was three and I remember getting out of the elevator where there were men all in white. I told them to wait for my mother, she was getting her pocketbook. That was the last thing I remember about that day.

The next earliest memory was running around a large room eating an apple and talking to a lot of adults who were lying in beds but not saying anything. I also remember standing in front of a store window, my mother's hand on my shoulder, looking at photographs of men wearing black eye patches and my mother asking me which I liked best. Obviously the experience made a deep impression on me.

As I was growing up, I recall dreading the moment when some kid would ask, "Hey, what's the matter with your eye—it looks funny—or how come one moves and the other don't." This sensitivity started decreasing in my early teens and was completely gone by high school. The kids were always electing me president. I felt comfortable with everybody and playing sports and being with the guys on the street corner and in poolrooms where everybody needled anybody about anything—it was a very healthy atmosphere for me. That's where I learned I could get a laugh.

———

At Ossining High School the baseball field was right in back of the school and the grandstand was very close to the playing field, particularly on the third base side. This is significant because on this particular day it was a play at third base where the umpire called me out. It was a bad call. I was clearly safe. I knew it and everybody in the stands knew it. They sat so close to the field, they could see and hear everything. In front of everyone, I whipped out my eye and handed it to the umpire: "You'll do better with this one." Talk about getting a laugh. I got a roar. Even the guys on the other team were rolling in the grass.

Peter, front row, second from left

I once went in for an eye test—you know, the one where you read the letters of the alphabet on a chart that's hanging on the wall. The guy conducting the test looked like he'd been doing this for *a lot* of years. To put it mildly, he was not too interested. He mumbled hello, indicated a chair. I sat down and he said, "We'll start with the left eye." So I covered the right eye and read the chart with my left, and he wrote down the numbers. He then said, "Now we'll do the right eye." I said, "The right eye is glass." He said, "Well, do the best you can."

The early eyes were all glass. The plastic ones didn't come in until the late '60s. When I was a kid, the doctors told me to make sure that every night I take out the glass eye and put it into a glass of water. Naturally, after doing this for sixteen years, you get sloppy—you forget—there's not a glass handy—you're drunk—you're tired, whatever. I would frequently just toss the eye under the pillow. There was a young lady I was attracted to who had a Pekingese, who sometimes slept with her. One night she afforded me the same privilege as the Pekingese. The following morning, I looked under the pillow—no eye. You guessed it! There was the Pekingese—a pig in shit—crunching away on my eye. Until they brought in plastic, that's the last time I slept in a bed that included a Pekingese.

Over the years, I went to four colleges—one of them was Hamilton. There, I got lucky with the four guys living across the dorm hall. They were extraordinarily funny, vital guys who introduced me to the world of ideas. For this story you need only know one of these guys—Pete Woitoch. A boy wonder physicist on a science scholarship, Pete played fabulous jazz piano. Art Tatum, at that time—and even now, fifty years later—is arguably the planet's number one jazz pianist. Tatum passed through Utica, New York, regularly, to play a local nightclub. Whenever he was there, he called Woitoch and invited him to sit in. I didn't know this. So the three guys came into my room, told me about Tatum, and the invitation for that night and how we were all going. I should have been thrilled, but I wasn't.

When I woke up that morning I couldn't find my eye. I remembered putting it down on an end table, but when I looked it wasn't there. I explained this to the guys and when I said I couldn't go, they wouldn't hear of it. "It's a nightclub—it's dark—nobody is looking at you. They're interested in Tatum, in themselves, in Woitoch—not in you." Actually, what they were saying made sense—I knew I could keep my lid closed and I was dying to go, so I relented. We headed out to the club.

What a great evening. The crowd loved Pete, so did Tatum, and when it got late and the place emptied, the five of us stood around the piano listening to Tatum play. Art liked his gin and usually had a jigger within reach. At one point, playing with only one hand, he slid the jigger in my direction. "I've had enough," he said, "help yourself—it's world-class gin."

I liked the idea of drinking Art Tatum's gin, so I lifted the jigger not to make a toast but as a gesture of gratitude in his direction. Then I noticed something at the bottom of the jigger; my glass eye—sitting there in the gin, at the bottom of that jigger—MY GLASS EYE!

Those sons of bitches—my buddies from across the hall—they had stolen my eye—and set me up. I can still see Tatum laughing—his shoulders shaking, the tears running down his cheeks—his hand reaching for a handkerchief wiping the water from his eyes. It was a beautifully crafted scam. I'll give 'em that.

my
wife
shera

I'VE BEEN ASKED a few thousand times how much of Columbo is Falk and vice versa. For years I've had a stock answer "I'm just as sloppy as the lieutenant but not nearly as smart." That was a quickie response for the media. They're drawn to anything that takes less than five seconds.

The truth is, no one is like Columbo. He's unique—if he were up for auction, he would be described as "One of a kind—a human with the brain of Sherlock Holmes who dresses like the homeless."

Having said that, however, I do share with the lieutenant one very pronounced part of his personality—he loves to talk about his wife. You can't shut him up. I have the same problem. I can tell Shera stories till three in the morning. Shera is my wife.

Cover of *Vanity Fair*, August 1991 issue: "Demi Moore, Naked and Pregnant"

Remember the nude photograph of Demi Moore on the cover of *Vanity Fair*? She wasn't wearing anything—nothing—no clothes—totally nude and PREGNANT. She looked fantastic. It was a dazzling photo of a sensationally beautiful woman in all her nude, pregnant glory. I saw it on the newsstand and immediately bought it.

I took it home and said to Shera, "I want to show you something." I handed her the magazine. "What do you think of *that*?" She took it—there was Demi on the cover—in all her naked splendor.

Shera's mouth opened, "Wow!! Look at that ring."

I never saw it—Shera never saw anything else—but sure enough, on her third finger the only thing Miss Moore had on was a big diamond rock.

thinking
about
faye dunaway
while
driving

I **HAD A** good feeling about the day's work. We'd filmed a scene between Faye Dunaway and Columbo in an upscale bar, where Faye's character asks, "Are we talking about Nick's apartment?" as if she didn't already know. She was feigning innocence, but she was doing it deliciously. Faye had a knack of delivering deception in such an absolutely convincing manner that it tickled Columbo—and brought a smile to my face. Just take a look at the photo.

The smile was a totally spontaneous reaction. I was enjoying the memory of it when I heard a police siren and saw a bright white light sweep across my windshield. I looked back and sure enough it was a cop. As I was getting out my registration I realized that in addition to thinking about Faye Dunaway, I had also been doing 55 in a 35-m.p.h. zone.

The cop ducked his head into the window on the driver's side. When he saw it was me, his mouth opened, his eyebrows shot up—"Oh my Lord, it's you—my wife *loves* you—I can't believe this—she *loves* you—wait till I tell her!"

This cop was astonished with delight. Even when he calmed down and was going through the police ritual ("Do you still live at this address?" etc.), he never let up telling me what a fan of the show his wife was. He even named her favorite clues as he returned my registration. When he paused to take a breath, he added, "You can mail this in or appear in court on the date that's marked. Either way is fine." I looked down and there in my hand along with my registration was the speeding ticket—$75.00. Now I was the one who was astonished—I wish I could say it was with delight. I looked back at the officer, just as he was getting into his car, he turned and give me the thumbs-up gesture, "You're the greatest."

Now, many years later, looking back at this guy—my hat's off to him.

NOTE TO THE READER

By now you should know what I like: short stories that can be read in ten minutes. Stories that grab the reader with an interesting beginning and lead to a surprise ending. Stories that supply a chuckle, that are designed for people like me, who pick up a book when they get into bed, read for 12 minutes, and doze off, hopefully with a smile on their lips.

However, there is a period in my life—a short period—only eleven years, beginning in 1945 when I graduated high school up to 1956 when I decided to become an actor, that pose a provocative question, i.e., "Why did it take me eleven years to decide to become an actor?" "Why did it take so long?" "What else was I doing that was so important?"

The answer to this question could be of interest to someone other than myself. I feel that most of us think about this aspect of our lives. We look back and wonder how we ended up where we are. What amazing luck, genes, and people combined to determine that one person ends up owning a key shop, another trains elephants, and a third sells shoes. Plus, in my case, for those eleven years what I did was so out of the ordinary—so kinda goofy—that I think it will be fun to write about and fun for you to read. So here goes.

on being
a young man
who has
no idea
what he wants
to do with his life

(p.s. and he is in
no hurry to find out)

I WAS 17, it was June of 1945, and when I left high school to go to Hamilton College there was one significant thing I didn't know. I didn't know what I wanted to do in life. There was also one thing I did know. I knew I had just finished a fabulous four years in high school and I knew college was going to be just as great.

Very early on at Hamilton College, maybe the first day, I realized that college was not going to be so great. First of all, there were *no girls*—I didn't know that—it was an all-male school! Secondly, there were very few males. It was wartime and when you hit 18, you got drafted—you went into the army, not to college. So the campus felt deserted and cheerless.

I grant you that someone with half a brain should have known these things. Knowing myself, my thinking wasn't complicated—

"There were boys and girls in high school, so there will be boys and girls in college." The reader is correct—I'm not dumb but a part of me is on the moon.

At any rate, not having a fixed goal and not having any fun, I didn't stay in college the full four years. I quit after three months and joined the Merchant Marine.

Men with one eye were not drafted and in the Merchant Marine they were not allowed to work on deck or below deck, but they could work in the kitchen. I sailed out as a third cook. My specialty was pork chops. We left New York, crossed the Atlantic for Marseilles, France, where we picked up two thousand soldiers. On the trip over I did nothing except rest up for the trip back. My duties on the return trip were to cook each day 400 pork chops for lunch. This was more than enough. It was winter and the seas were very high. The remaining 1600 soldiers were not interested in food—too busy barfing.

My sleeping quarters were a tiny cabin with two built-in platform beds. They called the room a bunk. There were two men to a bunk. I had the lower bed on the right side and my bunkmate had the upper bed on the opposite side. He was from northern California, a guy named Joe.

On my first night on the ship he was already in his pajamas looking down at me from his upper bunk. He lay up there without saying much, just watching me get undressed. At the time I had a removable bridge for my four upper front teeth. I took the bridge out and tossed it on the shelf next to my bed. The teeth made a little sound when they hit the wood. I then took out my eye, and tossed it on the shelf next to my teeth. That also made a little sound when it landed. I didn't have to look up to know that Joe was transfixed—his mouth open. What he had just seen, he had never seen before—a man reaching up to his face and using his fingers to dig into his socket and take out one of his eyes and then toss it onto a shelf. I then bent forward and put both hands on my

lower leg just below the knee. I adjusted myself, got my body in position where I could comfortably pretend to twist off my artificial leg. Before I had a chance to start turning, Joe hopped out of his bunk and headed for the door. "Excuse me," he said, "I think I'll get a little air."

Incidentally, Joe and a third guy, Chip, became buddies with me. In fact, the three of us signed up together for the next trip to South America.

Although I started out as third cook, I managed to work myself down to mess boy in less than four months. A year on the water was enough for me, so I returned to college. I didn't stay long. Too itchy. What to do next? I signed up to go to Israel to fight in the war with Egypt. I wasn't passionate about Israel. I wasn't passionate about Egypt. I just wanted more excitement.

Joining the Israeli Army was illegal for American citizens, but I found out you could sign up at the Hotel Roosevelt in Manhattan. I did and got assigned a ship and a departure date. However, the war, to everyone's amazement, was over in the blink of an eye—eight days, to be exact. The ship never sailed.

I was left high and dry with nothing to do (going to work never occurred to me). I decided I'd do some reading. I rented a room in Greenwich Village (Merchant Marine money—my father would pay for schooling, but not for reading), I got a lot of good books, a lot of Hemingway, Dos Passos, Conrad, Chekhov. For four months or so I was absorbed in them. Although I was in no hurry to find out what I wanted to do in life, sitting in a room and reading for four months started to feel odd. It was hard to explain to people and I felt if I enrolled in a school it would look to both the world and myself that I was headed somewhere.

So I signed up at a place called the New School of Social Research, which was only 15 minutes from where I lived. I majored in poli-sci and literature, but I didn't have the slightest idea how I was going to use the information outside the classroom. Reading the catalog, I discovered I could get credits toward my B.A. degree by being in a play. Apparently The New School was affiliated with a famous dramatic workshop.

Marlon Brando and Ben Gazzara were among the many future stars who trained there. Of course at the time I'd never heard of the place, but that's par for me. At that time I'd been in two plays. The first was when I was 13 at summer camp. The second, four years later, was in Ossining High School. It was a fluke. At the last minute, one of the kids in the senior class play got sick. As the class president, they came to me to save the day by filling in and taking over the sick kid's part. The play was a melodrama, *Double Door* by E. McFadden. My character only appeared in one scene. He was the detective that showed up in the last act and solved the mystery. That's God's truth, but if you're skeptical, call Ossining High School.

The New School explained to me that acting in a play was limited to advanced students. I would have to take preliminary classes. I tried to talk the director into letting me read for a part. He said no, but I kept after him and he finally agreed. I got the lead. The play was Saroyan's *The Time of Your Life.* And immediately after the opening night performance, the head of the school, world-renowned German director Erwin Piscator, offered me a scholarship. Without hesitation, I politely declined. That night in Louie's Tavern I told some buddies what had happened. I pointed out that what I did in the play was not real acting. It was all right, but compared to the real thing, it was nothing. And if Mr. Piscator thought differently, and he did, he was sadly mistaken.

Mind you, at that time I had only seen one Broadway play in my entire life. When I was 13, my mother took me to see *Bringing up Father*. What did I know about professional actors—nothing—but that didn't faze me. Despite Mr. Piscator, I knew that real actors were endowed at birth with some magnetic quality that the rest of us could only admire from our seats. I wasn't about to kid myself. Regarding the scholarship, I told the guys in the bar, "Case closed. Let others—let deluded people become actors and starve to death. Not me."

The reader may ask where did this naïve, romanticized, ridiculously unrealistic notion of what constituted a professional actor come from. It's a legitimate question. I'm not sure myself, but the bottom line is this: Standing on a street corner with the guys in Ossining, New York, it never occurred to any of us that we could be knighted by the Queen of England and in the same way, it never entered my consciousness that I could become a professional actor. Number one, actors were artists, and I thought artists were Europeans. I knew there were none in Ossining. As I previously mentioned—there's a part of me that's on the moon.

So there I am about to graduate college, and I don't know where I'm headed. But it sure wasn't acting.

i graduate college— next day paris

ICOULDN'T WAIT to graduate college. Not because it would take me a step closer to a career, but because I just wanted to get to Paris. There was an American girl there named Sheila, who was waiting for me. If you had asked me what I planned to do after I got to Paris, how long I planned to stay, I couldn't answer you. As far as I could see, the future didn't extend beyond the coming weekend. Whatever happened happened. I wanted to be with her, that's all I knew.

Well, something huge happened. Marshal Tito, the head man in Yugoslavia, told Josef Stalin, the mighty ruler of the Soviet Empire, to shove it. Sheila and I heard the news in Paris. At that time, nothing fascinated the Western world more than the mystery of what was happening behind the Iron Curtain. I'm not sure whose idea it was, but one of us said, "Let's go see." And the other one said, "Why not?" Gas up the jeep, get a bunch of sewing needles (we heard they were scarce in Yugoslavia and could be used to barter with), get Louie (the cocker spaniel), get a road map leading to the Yugoslavian frontier, and we were off.

Were we two airheads? No! Our curiosity was genuine. I was never one for sightseeing and this trip, thank God, wasn't about visiting museums. This was genuinely exciting. If we weren't the first Americans behind the Iron Curtain, believe me, there weren't many ahead of us. We could have gotten in a little earlier, but I got arrested in Trieste. It was stupid, I wanted to exchange some Italian money for some American money so I could buy dinars, Yugoslavian money. On the black market one dollar American bought you a bushel of dinars. But no one would take my Italian notes—I was told I had to wait until the banks opened on Monday to exchange them. To hell with waiting. I was annoyed. We went to a restaurant and I told the owner we'd be ordering food and drinks and to let me know when I hit an "X" amount of lira. He let us know. I handed him the Italian money. He shook his head, no good. I said, "That's all I have. Take it or leave it." He didn't do either; he called the cops. The polizia arrived and I got hot—Sheila had a big mouth—and I ended up in the clink.

At that time Trieste had a triparte administration—it was jointly governed by the Americans, the British, and the Italians. The following afternoon I'm sitting in my cell looking out the bars and who comes into view?—Sheila with an American military officer. A good man, he took the Italian bills, said he'd exchange them Monday at the bank, paid the restaurant with Italian money they would accept, and I was out in 20 minutes.

Alyce with Peter

Alyce with Yugoslavians

I was nervous about crossing that frontier with an illegal amount of dinars. You were only allowed to take in a limited amount. I didn't know what they would do, but I didn't want to test the waters. So I got a pair of secondhand paratrooper boots a couple of sizes too big and packed large-denomination dinars under the soles of my feet. At the frontier when I got out of the Jeep to show my passport, I was six foot two inches.

We stayed in Yugoslavia three to five months. Incidentally, the sewing needles were a Godsend—we used them to barter for gas and tire patches when we got flats, which was about once a week. There were no paved roads.

Sheila and I spent a month at a camp in Bosnia near Sarajevo, where we helped to build a railroad. An engineering background was not required. What we did was move rocks from point A to point B. It was one of Tito's favorite programs—kids from around the world responding to his invitation to lift rocks for three weeks in return for a week's free vacation. We had laughs at the camp. There were so many different languages, we had fun trying to communicate, plus we all had something in common: diarrhea.

The bloom was off the romance and I'm on a ship departing Naples and headed for New York. Naturally I felt different going back. Coming over it was exciting—a girl waiting in Gay Paree. Going back—nothing. No one waiting at the dock, but even worse, thinking beyond the dock to the next morning when I would get out of bed. How was I going to make a living? Obviously I had to make a decision regarding my future. Once again, going to work never occurred to me. Going back to school, however, felt right. "Continuing my education" had a nice ring to it. I didn't know what that meant, but the phrase by itself felt comfortable. The huge question for me was which subject to study. I picked public administration. Of all things, why a master's degree in public administration? I have no idea how that happened—but it did. I picked a program at Syracuse University that was new—the only one of its kind in the nation. It was limited to 30 students and was designed specifically to train people to work in Washington in the federal bureaucracy. I don't remember how I heard about such a program. I certainly didn't face the reality of the subjects I would be studying—I had absolutely no interest in any of them and no aptitude. But as they say, everything happens for a reason.

on working
to get a
master's degree
in a field
you have
no interest in
and no
aptitude for

AS WITH MY previous college experience, I drifted over to the drama department and got into a play. This time Shakespeare's *The Tempest*. I played the king's wise old counsel Gonzalo and a youth named Jerry Leiter played the king. For some reason, he didn't always allow enough time to glue on his beard properly. This is significant because I wanted to approach this pretty girl who worked *backstage* on the sets. But on this particular night, she came *on stage*—dressed as a sprite. One of the sprites got sick, and the pretty girl came on as a substitute sprite. In the scene where the sprites make a circle and dance around the king's company, I whispered to her as she passed me, "I'll give you a quarter if you pull the king's beard." When she returned as she danced by me, she whispered, "Up yours." Those were her first words to the man who later became her husband, and mine had been my first to the woman who later became my wife. When she danced by the third time, I asked Alyce out for coffee.

I had a terrific time at Syracuse University. First and foremost, there was Alyce. Also, I got lucky with Chip and Allan,* my roommates. However, the time was fast approaching when I would *actually* be working as a trained bureaucrat in the federal government. I never thought about that. It was too depressing. What life would be like as a bureaucrat in a federal agency in Washington was a question I was able to ignore until late May.

That was when all 30 of us in this special program would go on the much-anticipated crucial trip to Washington, D.C., to land our first jobs.

---

* Chip Forden and Allan Goldfarb. Also, Tom and Ann O'Connell. When Alyce and I got married Tom was best man at my wedding.

Alyce at Syracuse University

We would be ushered around the capital by the founder of the program, Mr. Paul Appleby. A highly regarded top player in the 12 years of the Roosevelt presidency,* Paul Appleby was known by everyone in Washington.

As the date of the trip drew near I had a sudden realization. Finally, one thing regarding my future crystallized that I could put it into words: I DID NOT WANT TO GO 9-TO-5 IN AN OFFICE.

Coming to that conclusion felt good, but it raised a huge question about my ever working in the federal bureaucracy. And that threw a black cloud over the coming trip to Washington. I didn't know how I could bring up my change of plans with Mr. Paul Appleby. What could he possibly say—he could only look at me in disbelief. I thought of pulling out of the Washington trip—just not going. Then it occurred to me that I had an option—an option that might work. In fact, the more I thought about it, the more it appealed to me: there will be no office, there will be no 9-to-5. I'll get involved in something exciting. "I'll go to work for the CIA—I'll get sent overseas—I'll become a spy."

My meeting at the CIA did not go as I'd planned. I remember the thick silence as I sat on one side of the desk watching this man peruse my resume. I knew he was highly placed and did not ordinarily interview job applicants. He was doing this as a favor to Paul Appleby. I don't remember if he addressed me as "son" or "Peter," but what he said went something like this:

CIA MAN
I, uh . . . don't know exactly how to tell you this, son—but uh . . . all right, let's start with your undergraduate schools—the first two, Hamilton College and Wisconsin University are

---

* Number two man in the Budget Bureau during the war. Number two man in the Agriculture Department before the war.

fine—no problem. However, the third—the one from which you received your degree—the New School of Social Research has a pinkish reputation and it doesn't get your resume off to a good start . . . and uh . . . going on . . . you were a member of the Marine Cooks and Stewards Union, were you not? (I shook my head yes.) Well, that union was a communist-dominated union . . . and, uh . . . finally let me say that in the history of the CIA you're the first and the only applicant that has a past that includes helping Marshall Tito build a railroad. So, uh . . . in all candor, Peter, you not only can*not* work for the CIA, you cannot work anywhere in Washington.

My career as a civil servant in Washington lasted 1 minute and 4 seconds. This was the beginning of the Joe McCarthy era, and the fact that I never met anybody from the union and signed up with the union in the first place only because the government put us guys in a truck and drove us to the union, didn't make any difference. But once again, as they say, everything happens for a reason—God bless that day and that meeting at the CIA.

With nowhere to turn, I was hired as an efficiency expert by the Budget Bureau of the State of Connecticut. On the first day, however, I couldn't find the office. The truth is, I wasn't exactly a crackerjack at the job I was hired to do, and I was doing exactly what I knew I was born not to do, i.e., go 9-to-5 in an office. But hallelujah, thank the Lord, I had ended up in Hartford, Connecticut, *the home of the MARK TWAIN MASKERS*, a community theater with a subscription list, a solid reputation, and a bunch of people who knew what they were doing. In my spare time, I did one play after another: works by Odets, Williams, Shaw, Miller. My real day started in the evening, when I left the budget office and went to rehearsal or to the theater to put on my costume and get ready for the 8 o'clock curtain. It took maybe a year and a half before the thought flickered across my mind that maybe I could be an actor, but it was gone as quickly as it came.

on the thin line dividing naïveté from stupidity, or why it took 12 years to become an actor

WHY DID IT take so long to decide to be an actor? Obviously fear—fear of failure, but fear by itself is too simple. It was fear coupled with my highly romantic, ridiculously unrealistic notion of what constituted an actor. What exactly do I mean by ridiculously romanticized? Let me explain. It's 1955, and by day I'm working for the budget director— I'm getting paid posing as an efficiency expert—and at night I'm an outstanding amateur actor, and I hear that a fellow that I went to Ossining High School with, Jimmy Cronin, *aka* Nicely Nicely Shamus,* has started, of all things, a winter repertory theater in New Haven, Connecticut. Could that be possible? I doubt it.

---

* Nicely Nicely refers to his golf swing—going back it was smooth and fluid. Shamus because he was Irish.

Nobody starts a winter repertory company, much less someone I went to high school with. I'm interested, but very skeptical.

I drive 45 minutes south from Hartford to New Haven. Holy jamolies, there's the theater, and to my amazed surprise and delight it's true. There's Jimmy's name and, not only that, he's presenting a play, *Bell, Book and Candle*. Even more exciting, I recognize the actors. Roddy McDowell, Maria Riva (Marlene Dietrich's daughter), Walter Abel, and Estelle Winwood are all well-known, established, name actors who have starred in movies and on Broadway. Wow! Maybe Jimmy is inside. I'd love to see him and hear how all this happened.

I go in and hear voices coming from the direction of the stage. There, in the orchestra, are four people talking. I suddenly stop. The figure standing is Roddy McDowell. No question about it. The three seated must be the other actors. This is a first—I have never before been in the same room—been in the presence of live professional actors. My first thought—*what are they saying?* I wanted to hear it. I was sure that whatever the topic they were discussing, it would be scintillating and lively with wit and sparkle, the like of which I had never heard before.

I started toward them down the aisle. My plan was to sit unobtrusively somewhere in their vicinity where I could both hear and not be noticed.

However, before I got seated they stood up. I didn't want them to see me looking at them so I turned away. They were headed outside. I followed at a discreet distance. When I got outside, I saw them turn right. I didn't know where they were going, maybe to a car. I broke into a casual trot. I wanted to hear their conversation before I lost them. But the street was noisy with traffic, and as I drew closer I felt if one of them turned and saw me I would look crazy. I slowed down, gave up any hope for now of actually hearing their words, and just followed them to see where they ended up.

I followed them for three blocks, and then they went into a drugstore where food was served. They took a booth, but I had to take a stool at the counter because the booths on either side of the actors were occupied. However, being at the counter made it difficult to hear anything. If I faced the counter, my back to the booth, I heard nothing. If I turned profile, my one ear facing them, I could only pick up an occasional word. I did my best moving my head to different positions and I did hear occasional words like "colonial," "view," "front," but only when they got up to leave and walked past me did I heard a whole sentence clearly, "If you want to make money in real estate, buy land in Los Angeles. That's what Bob Hope did." That's what I heard.

Obviously, that sentence did not have the wit I'd expected and I was deeply disappointed. But the point of the story is this: Is the person who turned these actors into storybook characters, that he would at the age of 26 surreptitiously follow down the street in the hope of catching snatches of their conversation because he believed it would have an unusual sparkle—is this person naïve or stupid? My wife would answer quickly—stupid.

Now remember, I actually followed these people—it really happened just as I described. My foolish innocence tickles me today, and I like me even though I'm dumb, so I only half-agree with my wife. However, putting aside the sparkling conversation notion and moving to the unrealistically high standards that I felt were required before someone could consider himself a real actor, these standards were intimidating. Who knows, maybe they would have intimidated Laurence Olivier. Bottom line, they made it extremely difficult for me to believe that I was born with the required combination of talent and personal magnetism. That's why my decision to become an actor dragged on for so long.

on the four words
that broke
the camel's back

WHAT PUSHED ME over the edge were four
words. But it wasn't just the words but the person who said them and the circumstances under
which they were said that did the trick. Eva LaGallienne was a towering figure in the American theater. She, along with Helen Hayes
and Tallulah Bankhead, was one of the three dominant Broadway
leading ladies of her time. LaGallienne was also a director, writer,
and founder of our nation's first repertory company. I read where
she was giving a summer course in Shakespeare restricted to professional actors at the White Barn Theater in Westport, Connecticut. By this time, I wanted to be on a stage and act with a
professional actor. I wanted to compare myself up close—I lied and
claimed I was a pro and got admitted. I told my boss that I wouldn't
be taking a summer vacation, but would like to take off every
Wednesday afternoon until September.

Eva LaGallienne

I didn't recognize any of the actors in the class. I assumed they were professionals, but when I compared myself, I didn't feel I should take a back seat to any of them. Just the opposite. I felt they were behind me. We were doing a production of *Richard III* and LaGallienne cast me as Richard. My problem was that I had to work in the mornings and then drive to Westport, so was frequently late for class. LaGallienne was a formidable, no-nonsense authoritarian with a passion for excellence. About the third time I was late, even before I hit my seat, LaGallienne froze me with a question: "Why are you always late?" I said I had to drive down from Hartford. She asked coldly, "What do you do there? There are no theaters in Hartford. How do you make a living?"

I told the truth. "I'm not an actor." She snapped back "Well, you should be, now sit down." I sat down, but not for long. I left class early. I didn't care if she saw me. I raced back to Hartford with "Well, you should be" ringing in my ears. I got back before the office closed, walked in to the boss, and quit. I'm going to be an actor.

the big apple
and my first play

I **WAS LUCKY** to land in New York at just the right moment. Those were exciting times for the off-Broadway theater. There was a hum in Greenwich Village, every month new theaters, new productions, and an eager audience—it was off-Broadway's heroic phase, and in a matter of weeks I got into a play—a production of Molière's *Don Juan*. I had a tiny part, maybe five lines, but I kept getting promoted and by opening night I was the second lead, playing Sganarelle, Don Juan's servant and right hand. Walter Kerr, the theater critic for the *Herald Tribune* and arguably our nation's preeminent theater authority at the time, opened his review with a note on my performance because, as Sganarelle, I opened the play: "Peter Falk got the evening off to a wonderfully paralyzed start with 10 minutes of totally unaccented exposition."

People ask how I reacted to such a review. The fact is, I agreed with him. I should have been crushed, but I knew what he wrote was true. In fact, the night before we opened, I bet the actor playing Don Juan twenty bucks that the play would be a bomb. If it (including my performance) had gotten good reviews, I would have been thrown. We deserved to be stoned.

I should note that that was the New World premiere of Molière's *Don Juan*. It had never been done on this continent before, and if that production had anything to do with it, it will never be done again. Incidentally the play ran for two hours—that was its entire run—one night.

the iceman cometh

TWO MONTHS LATER I got cast in Eugene O'Neill's *The Iceman Cometh**, directed by Jose Quintero. The difference between *Don Juan* and *The Iceman Cometh*— like night and day. *The Iceman* was fantastic, one of a kind. Here's why:

1. It ran 4½ hours—can you imagine!
2. The play was about drunks and the theater *was* an old bar.
3. It was a huge hit, maybe the biggest in off-Broadway history.
4. I played the bartender and had the first line, and for the next 4½ hours I never left the stage. It was hard to miss me.

---

* The play's title comes from the lead character's long-standing joke that he came home to find his wife in bed with the iceman: death.

The following is an inside story. Approximately every third performance, something happened on stage during the play that had never happened in the history of the theater and has probably never happened since. Let me explain—the play takes place in a combination saloon/flop house. There are the bartender, three whores, and 11 alcoholics who are seated with their heads resting on the tables in front of them—some are sleeping, others fitfully dozing, others just resting with their eyes closed, head in their arms, daydreaming. The only sounds are heavy breathing, mumbling, and an occasional cough. These guys have been drunk for years and every now and then for the next 4½ hours each one will come to life, lift his head, and say something—maybe make a speech—maybe answer what someone else said an hour earlier; but whatever they do, when they're finished, they return to their stupor, their heads hit the table, they're back in their dreamworld. The bartender is the only character totally awake and living in the present.

I remember vividly that particular performance when for the first time I was suddenly startled by a new totally unexpected sound—a rich, deep authentic snore. Holy jamolies. There is someone on this stage that is sleeping—*really* sleeping.

It was a good 65 feet from where I stood behind the bar to where the snore was coming from. I couldn't be sure, but I figured it was one of two actors—either Al Lewis or Conrad Bain—and I was nervous because if it was Al, who had a line coming up, I couldn't just dash down to his table. I had to make it look natural. I grabbed a broom and made believe I had to sweep. It turned out it was Al snoring. I rapped him upside his head—he woke up with a start—blinking. As the bartender, I told him, "Stop snoring. You're disturbing the other patrons."

Now would you believe on that same night, in the third hour of the play, another actor, Bill Edmonson, fell asleep? By the fifth month of the run, it was not at all uncommon for one or more actors sitting on

the stage in full view of the audience to be in a deep sleep. So in addition to playing my part, I had a second job—making sure every actor was awake when it was his turn to speak. The director insisted I keep the broom handy.

NOTE TO THE READER

Okay, it took eleven years, but I've finally arrived. I'm in the Big Apple playing a big part in a hit play. The journey is over. I finally know what I'm going to do with my life. I'm going to act—as my father would say, I'm going to "paint my face." Let's get back to the short stories. The next one is a honey. Whatever you do, don't pass up the next story—I guarantee you'll enjoy it.

jason robards
tells a good story

IN ADDITION TO being a hell of an actor, Jason had another distinction: No actor—living or dead—could interpret Eugene O'Neill better than Jason. Similar to Joe Mantegna's uncanny ability to step into and become one with any David Mamet character, Jason owned O'Neill. No one else came close.

The character Jason played in *Iceman* was the biggest drunk in a play full of drunks. Likewise, Jason himself (and this is no secret) had a well-oiled elbow and spent his share of time in bars. Sitting in a bar one night, he told me the following story.

There was an advertising executive who commuted from his office on Madison Avenue to his home in Connecticut. He was a big drinker, but that never stopped him—sloshed or not—from driving up the Connecticut Turnpike to his home.

One night he got so plastered at an office party that everyone begged him not to make the drive. He insisted, saying that he was fine, nothing to worry about. Off he went.

He was halfway home, probably weaving pretty good, when a cop blasts him with a spotlight, makes him pull over and get out of the car. Right then there was a traffic accident on the other side of the turnpike. A couple of cars headed into the city got tangled up in the southbound lane. It looked serious. The cop ran toward the accident, yelling to our hero, "Stay put. I'll be right back." After a couple of minutes, the ad man felt he had waited long enough. To hell with it. He climbed back in the car and was on his way home.

Once in the house he told his wife he was going to sleep. If anyone came looking for him, he instructed her, tell the person he was sick in bed and the doctor had ordered him not to be disturbed.

Early the next morning—ding, dong—the doorbell rings. The wife opens the front door to find two state troopers standing there. They ask for her husband, and she explains he's been sick and the doctor has ordered that he not be disturbed. The troopers hear her out, take a beat, then one of them asks, "Will you follow us, ma'am, this will just take a minute." They head toward the garage to find the door wide open. The wife stops—her mouth opens: there in the middle of the garage sits a black-and-white.

on being an actor
with one eye

AFTER KNOCKING AROUND off-Broadway for two years, something unexpected happened. I got a job on a TV show. I don't remember much about the character but, unlike my period costumes on the stage, I must have worn a contemporary suit because a talent scout from Columbia Pictures said, "This kid is a young John Garfield—sign him up." Well, that sounded good and I told the agent to grab it.

The deal was all worked out, my agent and I were only waiting for Harry Cohn, the legendary head of Columbia Pictures, to come to New York and give his personal okay. (Cohn had to okay everything—even the purchase of string.) My agent was an enthusiastic young lady and she opened the meeting with Mr. Cohn by pointing out that, "Yes—it is true Peter is a young John Garfield, but it's important for you, Mr. Cohn, to know that he is also a versatile actor and has done the plays of O'Neill, O'Casey, and Christopher Fry."

Mr. Cohn's answer in the form of a question was designed to put an end to the subject of versatility: "Young lady, do you think I care if Marilyn Monroe can play an old lady?" He then looked me straight in the face and said something that bewildered me: "Young man, I'm concerned about your deficiency."

I had no idea what he meant. To me, if you weren't getting enough vitamins, you had a vitamin deficiency. I didn't think I had a vitamin deficiency, but even if I did, how would he know? I said, "I don't know what you mean."

He looked as though he wasn't sure that I was telling the truth. He must have felt that this was a sensitive subject for me, so he replied gently, "I think you do know what I'm referring to." I said again I had no idea.

Finally he came out with it—"I'm concerned about your eye."

"Oh, that—that's nothing. Not to worry. No problem."

I had lived with one eye for 24 years, and the chances are I couldn't tell you if you caught me off guard and suddenly asked which one was glass and which one was real—I couldn't tell you—I'd have to test it—I'd have to cover one with my hand. I never—*but never*—thought about it, and I was convinced that the eye wouldn't be a problem. And I told him all this and asked bluntly why it hadn't been a problem for his talent scout.

He pointed out that TV is a small screen and movies are a big screen, and he wanted me to take a screen test. *WELL, I DID NOT* want any part of a screen test and I got a little hot and kept arguing—kept telling him he was wrong—he was making a big deal out of nothing—when he suddenly ended the conversation—he cut me off in midsentence with: "Young man, for the same price I'll get an actor with two eyes."

P.S.: I took the screen test. I failed. I went back to off-Broadway.

Peter as "a young John Garfield"

marjorie morningstar

THE FIRST FIVE years that I became an actor I like to call my off-Broadway Greenwich Village period. Going from one small 100-seat theater to another. Not getting rich. $10 a week for rehearsal and $30 when the play opens—not a lot left over for dinner at the Waldorf.

There were occasional TV shows, and I had a couple of lines in a disaster movie. The movie, to be clear, wasn't about a hurricane; the disaster was at the box office. In terms of name recognition— among the American public—it was definitely low. However, I wasn't a total unknown, I did have a certain following. There was my mother and father, there were the girls from Ossining High School and my cousin in Jersey. Nothing to write home about, but better than nothing.

Knowing this, you can imagine my excitement when my agent called to say that I had a meeting with the director and producer of a movie. Not any movie—oh, no—a big, hot ticket, blockbuster based on a best-selling book, *Marjorie Morningstar,* starring Natalie Wood and Gene Kelly. The coming season's hottest item.

I arrived at the appointed office ten minutes early, was told to take a seat, and 15 minutes later was told they'd see me now. It was a large room and as I walked toward the two men, one of them leapt out of his chair.

FIRST MAN
(excited, pumped up, to the second man)
Marty look, can you believe this? Look—he's perfect—the height, the hair—everything—perfect. Are you an actor?

PETER
Yes.

FIRST MAN
(delighted)
Even the voice, Marty. Unbelievable.
Say it again, "I'm an actor."

PETER
I'm an actor.

FIRST MAN
Perfect. Marty, the way he stands, the hair—Marty, the hair!
You have an agent?

PETER
Yes.

FIRST MAN
What's the name?

PETER
Isabel Baker.

FIRST MAN
We'll be in touch. I can't get over it. Just walks in and there
he is, our third lead. You ever work?

PETER
Yes. Mostly plays. Right now. . .

FIRST MAN
That's fine. Sounds good. Okay, good, we'll contact your
agent. Thanks for coming in.

I'm in the lobby, virtually walking on air. I called my agent immediately. She wasn't in, so I left a message. "Terrific meeting—they'll be calling you. I'll be in my apartment. Call me as soon as you hear."

Later in the afternoon I was in my apartment and the phone rang.
It was my agent.

AGENT
I got the call.

PETER
What did they say?

AGENT
They said you weren't right for the part.

I was stunned—couldn't believe it. I had to sit down—couldn't move. That happened—just the way you read it—there's no business like show business.

leo penn's ad-lib

THE BEST AD-LIB I've ever heard was from Leo Penn in 1956. Leo was a terrific actor in New York, who married a fabulous actress, Eileen Ryan. He and Eileen produced Sean Penn and Chris Penn, two fair country actors.

Leo and I were cast in a live TV show in the 1950s. In live TV, an actor had only one chance to get it right—no retakes; if you screwed up, the whole country saw it. So you had to be pretty confident to make up a line on the spot and throw it out there with all of America watching—but that's what Leo did.

In the show, Leo played a dimwitted character who stopped by my apartment for a visit. The scene took place in my living room. At the last minute just before shooting, the set decorator spruced up the room by adding some photographs, including one of the Mona Lisa. During the scene Leo, seeing the picture for the first time, turned and asked, "Your mother? Pretty woman."

on my wedding day

I **GATHERED THE** family in Grandma's very small kitchen. I had an important announcement: come June, Alyce and I would be married. My grandmother (Oma) usually had to repeat everything to Pop-pop in order to help him understand what had been said. He was in his late eighties and his faculties were not what they used to be.

"Did you hear?" Oma asked Pop-pop. "Peter is getting married to Alyce. They're being married in June."

Pop-pop smiled and nodded—he understood and was pleased. About 20 minutes later, Pop-pop was standing in the doorway, holding a pair of black patent-leather dress shoes. Oma asked him, "What are you doing with those shoes?" Pop-pop said he was going to Peter's wedding.

"In June, Pop. It's only February. Peter gets married in June," she said.

Peter's grandparents

"In June?"

"Yes, June. You have plenty of time."

Pop-pop arrived in the doorway only once more that night with his dress shoes ready to go to my wedding. However, in the months that followed, Pop-pop sometimes arrived in the doorway ready to go to the wedding twice a day.

Finally, the big day comes. The procession has marched down the aisle. My best man, Tommy O'Connell, has handed me the ring, and Alyce and I are about to step forward to take our vows. Suddenly I hear voices. I turn and see Oma and Pop-pop in the first row.

POP-POP
What's going on here?

OMA
Shhh—Quiet!

POP-POP
What's going on?

OMA
Peter is getting married.

POP-POP
Which one is Peter?

Peter's father

my father

YOU MIGHT RECALL my father's reaction to the news that I wanted to become an actor: "You mean you're going to paint your face and make an ass of yourself for the rest of your life?"

He shook my hand and wished me luck—but he was obviously just trying to put on a good face. For him, it was not only an odd way to spend your life—to be an actor!—who would even think of such a thing—but maybe more important, he's asking himself, "How's this kid going to eat?" It's a known fact that most actors starve to death. So from that point forward, the first questions were always the same: "So what's new? What's happening? Any jobs? A nibble? Something? What?"

Now if I said I got a job, he asked the same question every time: "How much are they paying you?"

I'd tell him, "$30 a week." His response never varied—he didn't speak. No answer. He'd just put his head in his hands, and rub his brow. That same ritual was repeated each time we saw one another.

Then something wonderful happened that changed everything.

PETER

Good news, Pop. I got a part in a movie.

FATHER

How much does it pay?

PETER

$500 a week.

FATHER

Say that again.

PETER

(chuckling) $500 a week.

It was a terrific moment. He was beaming. Naturally my father wanted to hear all about it. I told him the movie was going to be shot in the Florida Everglades—that it was a period picture set around 1900—and that it would start shooting this coming Monday and I would fly down Sunday.

FATHER

Here's what I want you to do. You start work on Monday. At the end of that week, on Sunday, call me. I want to hear if they like what you're doing for them, if they're happy with your work. So call me.

Naturally, I agreed.

A word about this movie. . . . It was *NOT* your traditional Hollywood studio film. In fact, I don't recall there being any studio involved and don't know where they even got the money to make it. *Wind Across the Everglades* is to this day my strangest acting experience ever. Only two professional actors in the cast: Christopher Plummer and me. The rest were an odd assortment of celebrities, including Tony Galento, one of the world's top prizefighters who had fought Joe Louis for the heavyweight championship; Sammy Resnick, a jockey who won the Kentucky Derby; Gypsy Rose Lee, our nation's most celebrated stripper; and McKinley Kantor, a renowned Civil War historian. With a cast like that, you know you're going to be in for some interesting times ahead.

It was a period picture set in the early twentieth century. The story centers around a gang of outlaws who kill birds in the Florida Everglades, then sell their feathers to the Parisian fashion market as plumes for expensive women's hats.

Obviously, birds played a large part in the story and provided the reviewer for *Time* magazine with the hook he needed to write a succinct review. It read, and I quote: "This movie is about birds and it's for the birds." That was it. I didn't leave a word out. Boy, I should have seen that one coming.

When the movie started shooting on Monday, the schedule was changed and suddenly I wasn't needed that day. Since I now had the day off, I played golf. It turns out they didn't finish Monday's work on Monday, so Tuesday I was on the golf course again. Then they told me the schedule for the remainder of the week would be changed and as of now I wouldn't be needed until the following week.

The situation was pleasant. I had a comfortable room. They paid me my per diem, encouraged me to relax, play golf, whatever, and they would check with me the beginning of the next week.

On Sunday I called my father as I had said I would. He of course wanted to know if the people in charge were happy with my work. I explained to him that I hadn't worked yet.

FATHER

What do you mean, you didn't work?

That's what you're there for. What else would you do?

PETER

I played golf.

FATHER

Don't get smart, Peter.

PETER

I'm not being—

FATHER

Never mind. Just be quiet. They told you to be there on Sunday. Were you there? Yes or no.

PETER

Yes.

FATHER

And on Monday what happened? You overslept?

PETER

No. They changed the schedule.

They shot another scene.

I wasn't in it.

FATHER

But they told you to be there on Sunday, correct?

PETER

Yes.

FATHER

And you were there on Sunday? Yes or no.

PETER

Yes.

FATHER

So what did they have you do on Monday?

You carried things? You brought the food in? What?

PETER

I told you.

FATHER

What?! You told me what?

PETER

I played golf.

FATHER
Golf?

PETER
That's right—every day—six days—golf.

FATHER
(*Long pause; calmly but firmly*)
All right. Here's what you do. You go to the guy—the first
thing to straighten out—number one—your room and
board. You want to see the room bill. What room are you in?
Never mind—not important—you want to see it—the bill—
you want a copy marked paid. And per diem—$25 per
week—you gotta eat. Are these people crazy? You gotta get
some food money. You gotta go to the guy—get it straightened out.

PETER
I got the per diem, last Sunday, the day I arrived. $35. And
tomorrow I'll get a check for $500 for the first week.

FATHER
(*Quietly but firmly*)
Listen to me, Peter, listen carefully. You're smarter than
me—you went to college—you have a degree—you read
books, so on and so forth—but listen to me—one thing I'm
telling yuh—They are not—you hear me?—They are not paying you $500 a week to play golf. Go to the guy, get it
straightened out—the room and board—call me tomorrow.

Well, for three weeks they didn't get to me. I played golf. I had to send him the signed receipts for the cashed checks. He was stunned—went all over town telling people, "Is this a good country or what?! The kid plays golf every day for seven days and at the end of the week they pay him $500." He's grinning—my father—he's laughing, his sides are shaking, "I'll be a son of a bitch. Is that business—that movie business—is that a good business or what?"

i have never been arrested in the united states but i have been arrested in . . .

I **HAVE NEVER** been arrested in the United States but I have been arrested in Paris, Moscow, Havana, Genoa, Belgrade, and Trieste (after the war when it was administered by the Americans, the British, and the Italians).

Let's start with Havana, 1958. I was shooting *Wind Across the Everglades* in Florida. It was a period picture (turn of the century 1900–1910). My character—true to that period—wore an outlaw's beard and moustache, and my hair was left long and unruly.

My part was tiny—for me I wasn't making a movie—I was playing golf. So one day I decided to check out Havana. It was a quick flight from Miami, and in no time I was at my hotel. The weather was glorious and I couldn't wait to take in the sights.

However, I got no more than a few blocks from the hotel when a car screeched to a stop alongside of me. The doors flew open and three men leapt out, running in my direction. Without a word they slammed me into a wall then threw me face down on the ground. One of the men held down my head, while another grasped my feet and the third cuffed my hands.

What was happening to me was so fast and frightening that I thought I might be killed. I was therefore relieved to see us pull up at a police station and discover that these were cops. A bewildering period of questioning followed. They spoke only Spanish, which I didn't understand a word of. They didn't beat me, but I was still so shook up from the arrest that I wasn't sure they wouldn't try. They had my wallet with American money and my California driver's license. From time to time they spoke among themselves; men left the room while others came in, phone calls were made.

They also found my hotel room key in my pocket. Suddenly we were back in the car and headed to the hotel, where they interrogated the desk clerk. I still had no idea what was happening. I asked the clerk. He said they wanted him to identify me as the person who had checked into the hotel. "They think you're with Castro," he added. "Castro?" I asked, flabbergasted. "Si, Fidel."

I had heard of Castro. I'd heard of Che Guevara, too. I knew they were revolutionaries—I knew they were Communists and there was fighting in Cuba. But what I didn't know, and what the desk clerk explained and what immediately made sense out of this nightmare, was that Castro and his men were in the hills just a few miles outside of Havana. The government was expecting an attack in a matter of days; in fact, some revolutionaries had already infiltrated the city.

That's where I come in: all of Castro's men, like Castro himself, wore black beards, a moustache, and a mop of black hair. If you look at the photo of me below, the police response makes perfect sense. To these guys I'm the terrorist on the plane.

I didn't hang around Havana. I was gone that afternoon, and three weeks later Castro and his men came down from the hills, captured Havana, and took over Cuba.

Peter in *Wind Across the Everglades*

murder, inc.

UNLIKE **WIND ACROSS** the Everglades, Murder, Inc. was a script of substance. It had started off as a book written by New York City district attorney Burton Turkis. Our country was stunned—shocked, in fact—to discover that murder was a business. That there actually was a gang that other gangs could hire for murder. That murder was their specialty. You gave them the name, paid the money, and these gangsters would, as they colorfully put it, whack the guy.

The most prominent member of "Murder, Inc." was a hood, also colorfully referred to as, Abe "Kid Twist" Reles. I played "Kid Twist."

The movie Murder, Inc. was no big deal for Twentieth Century Fox. They hired second-tier stars, nobody had ever heard of them. The cast of off-Broadway stage actors, including me, came cheap. A few dollars a week and a bag of peanuts.

However, for me *Murder, Inc.* was more than a big deal—it was a miracle. Like being touched from above. Of all the thousands of obscure actors, they picked me. That movie made my career. Without *Murder, Inc.* I wouldn't have gotten *Pocketful of Miracles* or later the Sinatra/*Robin and his Seven Hoods* combo. I'd still be kicking around off-Broadway.

I had a terrific agent. His name was Bill Hart, he got me *Murder, Inc.* It's that simple. He did it. He and the director, Stuart Rosenberg. Bill also handled Stuart and brought Stuart to a TV set where I was playing a gangster in a jail cell. I think what Stuart saw was a rehearsal—whatever it was, he hired me. And the next day I was on the hunt for the right hat and topcoat. I didn't know from costume designers. In the off-Broadway theater, I brought my own costume from home. I was obsessed, going from one small secondhand clothing store to another. Finally, bingo!—the right hat with the brim turned up and then that perfect coat with those perfect high shoulders that reduced your neck to nothing—and the topper, the reddish brown color. That was it—the urban East Coast "wise guy" look.

I had a real feel for these guys—the way they talked—the gestures—the whole package. I had spent hours in a pool hall named McGuires. I virtually lived there. At any hour of the day, McGuires was full of "would-be wise guys." You'd hear the now-famous "F'git-about it" every three minutes. The "would-be's" came from the same neighborhoods as the real wise guys—they were perfect copies, only they weren't the real thing.

Right from the get-go, I rewrote my part . . . new attitudes, new scenes—the whole nine yards. Stuart, thank the Lord, wasn't checking the script. He was a top-notch director who reacted to how the movie played, not whether the script was being followed word by word. What he liked he would leave alone—and he liked the bulk of what I did.

Just when I felt like I was nailing this character, BANG, something unexpected happened. The actors are going on strike. The strike would start in a few weeks, and the movie would be shut down. Word came from the West Coast—*Finish the movie before the strike.* Stuart was ordered to speed up and *finish the picture no matter what.* The next day, he went 30 percent faster. He was fired that night. I couldn't believe it.

The movie's producer was named the new director. He was a member of the family that owned Twentieth Century Fox. He was a very likeable man, but he had no experience. He had never directed before. In fact, it felt like he was feeling his way even as a producer. To his credit he stayed out of the way. He let us—the production man, the director of photography, and myself—run the ship.

Vincent Gardenia, Simon Oakland, and Peter Falk

courtesy of Photofest

I didn't think we would make it. Nobody else did either. No director plus a killer schedule meant it would take a miracle to pull this thing off.

Somehow we got to the last day. We had until midnight. At the stroke of 12, the lights go off—the movie is shut down.

One of the scenes scheduled for shooting that day was a murder. The murder took place in upstate New York outside a scenic summer resort in the Catskill Mountains. Morey Amsterdam, a comedian working at the resort, was stabbed to death in broad daylight by my character. In addition to that, we also had a ton of other scenes to do. Obviously we weren't driving to upstate New York.

We were headquartered and scheduled to shoot an interior scene that day at our sound stage on 126th Street in Harlem. When I asked what we were going to use for the Catskill Mountains, Tom, the production man, said that 30 miles north in Westchester County there was some wooded terrain and an old inn that we would use. It got to be around 1 P.M. and we still had a lot of work to do. I asked Tom how he felt about the 30-mile trip to Westchester. He shook his head, "We can't make that trip, but I have a backup that should be fine. It's much closer, about nine miles. There's no building there, but we'll figure something out."

We went back to work. We were moving furiously, but we had a location snafu that held us up. It's eight o'clock and we've clearly lost the light. I asked again about the murder and Tom said, "It's now a night scene and right there—you see that bridge?—On the other side of the water there's a park with a tree and two benches—that's the Catskill Mountains." That's it.

It's now 10:45—we've only got an hour—we've just finished shooting outside a five and dime—we roar to the soundstage—the whole circus—trucks, cars, crew, cameras. We rush inside to do our interior scene—start lighting, start blocking, actors half-dressed changing wardrobe—no makeup—no close-ups—no second chances. It's 11:45—

we're finished inside—Tom and a camera guy rush madly for the exit yelling, "The murder scene, quick!"

Morey and I follow, yelling, "Where?"

Tom says, "Right here."

We're on the sidewalk. There's traffic. They're moving trashcans. There's a crew guy on the hood of a parked car holding up a light. The union guy is there—he's got his watch out. He says if the camera's rolling, he'll let us go until we cut the shot. Tom yells, "Action"—we say a couple of lines, I take out the knife and stab Morey in the stomach. Morey falls—hits the sidewalk. Tom yells, "We're still rolling, do it again." I get the knife ready—Morey's not moving—I bend down—Tom shouts, "Morey, we're still rolling." Morey's dazed. His head is cut and I help pull him up. He repeats his last line—I say mine—knife in the stomach—Morey falls. *CUT.* We're out of film.

But we made it. A city sidewalk became the Catskill Mountains.

Regarding what you just read. . . .

Looking back at it, who would dream that what emerged from that chaos and confusion would be an Academy Award nomination. As they say in Brooklyn—"go figure."

on my first meeting with frank capra

GROWING UP, MY favorite pictures, like everybody else's, were those of Frank Capra. John Cassavetes, looking back, observed, "Maybe there was no America—maybe there was just Frank Capra."

Anyway, it's 1961. The TV industry had abandoned New York City and moved to Hollywood. Hordes of actors from Bohemian Greenwich Village, myself included, rushed to migrate to the West Coast. We came by train and plane and thumb—it was Hollywood or bust.

Los Angeles was a whole new world to me. Most men had proper haircuts. There was no off-Broadway theater. No guys on the corner hawking newspapers. No subways but plenty of freeways. Plenty of sun, too.

I hadn't even unpacked when Abe Lastfogel, the legendary agent, called me in to his office. "Peter, you got off to a good start with that *Murder, Inc.* I'll show it to Frank Capra. He might have something for you. In the meantime, go and see him."

The meeting with Capra got off to a bad start. I was no good at small talk. Capra was worse. I was nervous but wanted very badly to make a strong impression, so I asked, "Mr. Capra, do you read people?" That's how actors in New York got jobs in those days. You went to an address, you were given a script to study for twenty minutes, they brought you before the director, you read the scene aloud, and they said yes-no-maybe. That's what I wanted from Capra: a chance to read.

But when I asked the question, Capra looked at me funny, as if he'd been thrown. I thought maybe he hadn't quite heard me so I repeated my question. "Mr. Capra, do you read people?" Well there was no ambiguity this time. He was visibly uncomfortable and shook his head, mumbling no. End of meeting.

Capra saw *Murder, Inc.* and liked me. To my amazement, my second picture was his *Pocketful of Miracles*, starring Bette Davis and Glenn Ford. Soon, Capra was easy to be with. And after a month or so, I felt confident enough to bring up the subject of our meeting. "Mr. Capra, do you recall our first meeting? When I asked you the question, 'Do you read people' you became very uncomfortable? Why?"

Frank nodded his head, making it clear that he remembered the exchange. He smiled. "Peter, when you asked me do I read people, I thought you meant do I read people's palms."

No wonder he was ill at ease. Capra was thinking, here's a kid straight out of New York who's saying that the lines in the palms of his hands would tell whether he's the actor for the job. After this introduction, it's a wonder I got the part.

on wanting to kiss frank capra

THE FIRST DIRECTOR I wanted to kiss smack on the lips was Frank Capra. The film was *Pocketful of Miracles*. I have one especially fond memory of making that picture. It also illustrates what working with an extraordinary director like Frank Capra was like. *Pocketful of Miracles* is a comedy about a boss gangster played by Glenn Ford. I'm part of his mob; my character is Joy Boy, who got the nickname because he's easily annoyed. The life of a gangster can be a difficult one; there are pitfalls and he has no patience for them.

One scene takes place in the foyer of a magnificent Park Avenue penthouse. Joy Boy is fed up with an English butler, played by the inimitable Edward Everett Horton, one of the all-time great character actors. Joy Boy is uncomfortable being inside a swanky penthouse, a situation made worse by the presence of this impeccably

Peter and Frank Capra

proper English butler. Joy Boy is so busy ranting at everybody and everything that he can't manage to get his arm through the sleeve of his overcoat. His arm keeps getting stuck and the butler's earnest attempts to assist him only make matters worse.

We shot the scene three or four times, with each new take worse than the one before. Finally Frank called out, "Peter, get some coffee—we'll take a break." Fifteen minutes later, Frank was back in his director's chair and yelled action. We began the scene and, to my surprise—WHAT A TAKE—IT WENT LIKE A DREAM. Funny. But effortlessly funny. Not forced. It tickled me as I was doing it. What happened? What made the difference? Simple. During the break, Capra had the wardrobe lady sew up the lining in the sleeve of my overcoat. Using that needle and thread—that *one* thing—removed all the fake from the scene. Frank knew that my problem was faking something that was very simple to do—that anyone could do—like getting one's arm through a sleeve of an overcoat. He fixed that. There was no hole in the sleeve. The arm couldn't go through. I could have kissed him. And I could have kissed him again when I heard the news that I had another Oscar nomination. Truly, one of my happiest working experiences in the movies.

on the role overcoats can play in an actor's career

WHEN I WAS hired for *Murder, Inc.*, I became obsessed with finding the right overcoat. East Coast big-city hoods had a special look. I spent three weeks on the Lower East Side going to secondhand used clothing stores and finally found the perfect coat. It was a rich reddish brown with big shoulders that raised your own shoulders to just below your ears thereby reducing your neck. That was a characteristic of mafia wise guys. They all had short necks. You look at photographs and invariably they had high shoulders and squat necks. I don't ever recall seeing a wise guy with an elegant neck.

Anyway, the first time out of the blocks, wearing that coat produced an Academy Award nomination. Now the next picture is a comedy, but I'm playing a mobster again. I tell Frank Capra I've got the perfect coat (I didn't say it's from *Murder, Inc.*) and he says wear it. What-uh you know? We (the coat and I) get another

Oscar nomination—What a start! Me and the coat go two for two—first two pictures, two nominations—unheard of. Unfortunately, for the third picture I select a movie that's being shot in Russia. (Don't ask me why—career-wise it's not a shrewd choice.) Plus it's a World War II Army story, so obviously I can't wear a mob guy's overcoat—in fact, I don't wear any overcoat. The streak is broken—the movie played in L.A.—four people saw it.

However, fast-forward seven years and I'm about to play a homicide detective named Columbo. I remember that six years earlier on 57th Street in Manhattan, I had bought a raincoat. I always felt comfortable in that raincoat, and I liked its length—short, hitting just above the knee. It popped into my mind that the raincoat might be good for this character. I felt that Columbo should be drab—the raincoat was no problem in that regard. I think it's fair to say that this coat was an important part of the character's appeal. Without it, who knows?

The raincoat worked 76 episodes for almost 27 years, but in the late '90s we became concerned. It started to look fragile. I did what I could. Each evening, I put out a saucer of milk for it. The media claims it's now in the Smithsonian. If my second-floor closet is the Smithsonian, they're right—that's where it is. And thank heaven, still intact—still ready to go. However, it's a legitimate question: how would my career have been affected without those coats?

Peter as Abe "Kid Twist" Reles in *Murder, Inc.*

making a movie in russia—why?!

IT'S 1962. I'VE made my first two pictures, I've got two Oscar nominations—I ask all my friends "How long has this been going on?" Now I'm about to choose my third picture. My selection stuns my agent. I picked a picture that was to be shot in Russia, of all places. "How dumb can you be?" my agent wondered. Mind you, this is at the height of the Cold War. People have asked me, "Why, after such a good start, would you choose to get lost for five months in Russia?" Well, it wasn't the script— that's for sure.

The truth is, I was curious. Just like ten years earlier when, in 1952, Sheila and I raced for the Yugoslavian frontier the day after Tito broke with Stalin. Winston Churchill said it best: "Russia is a mystery wrapped in a riddle inside an enigma." Well, for the curious, what more can you ask?

We land in a primitive rural farm town in the Ukraine named Poltava. Making this picture was an odd experience from the beginning. The film was an Italian–Russian coproduction, and the head honcho was a well-known Italian director. The first night in Poltava, Alyce and I were invited to join the director for dinner. It turned out that his apartment was a tiny island of western civilization. He had brought from Rome lovely demitasse cups, his favorite olive oil, a beautiful Yugoslavian mistress, an ascot, and the finest espresso. He seemed to find me an unusually interesting person. He gave me his undivided attention. He would lean into me as he asked me questions.

DIRECTOR

Peètur—tell me—you know Frank Sinatra?

PETER

[Nods yes.]

(I'd once spent 12 minutes with him.)

DIRECTOR

(*To his mistress in the kitchen*)

Natasha—Come—Peètur, talk Frank Sinatra—

Whatever I said seemed to fascinate him. When I finished, he nodded thoughtfully. Natasha was getting up to return to the kitchen, but the director gestured to her to wait.

DIRECTOR

Peètur—tell me—you know Mafia?

PETER

[Nods yes.]

DIRECTOR
Natasha, sit—Peètur, talk Mafia.

The evening was over, and on the way back to our room I mentioned to Alyce how comfortable the director made me feel. Alyce turned to me and said, "He doesn't like you." I couldn't believe my ears.

The next day, Alyce and I were strolling down the street when an old cab pulled up beside us and stopped. It was a very old car, but it turned out to be from the movie company. The Russian driver, via sign language, indicated we should get in. He then drove us to a farm. Cutting through a wheat field, I saw a dirt road and on it two Russian men approaching us. One carried a little wooden stool and the other had a brown paper bag.

They indicated that I should sit on the stool, which I did; then they handed me a little cracked mirror. I felt something being pulled over my head. It must have come out of the paper bag. It felt like a wig. I looked in the mirror. It was a blond wig. When I saw Alyce laughing, rolling hysterical in the wheat, I knew that my head with that blond mop on it would never again be seen by another human. I tore it off.

Next thing I know, the picture shut down. No shooting—the entire crew just hanging around. No one seemed to know what the problem was. A couple of nights later, there was a sudden sharp knocking on my door around 2:00 a.m. It's the line producer with bad news: The director refuses to continue the picture with me in the role. Excuse me?—Did I hear right? He repeats it—the director will not make the picture with me in the role. It's nothing personal, but I'm too mature for the part. The director is adamant—the role requires someone more innocent, more boyish—in his words, "a bambino." Then why was I picked in the first place? The producer explained that I was hired off of my photograph— an 8 x 10 glossy headshot. And get this—off that same photo, the director thought he was getting Sal Mineo. Can you imagine? (Here's the photo.) There's no business like show business.

So here's the situation. The director doesn't want me in the role. What the director doesn't know is that I think the role is dumb. I couldn't care less. I only came here out of curiosity. Now the producer wants to know—that's putting it mildly—he's actually begging—if there's another part in the picture that I would like to play. This is crucial for him because if I'm not in the picture, he will lose the $200,000 that the American distributor (Joe Levine) put up for the American rights. Naturally I don't tell the producer the truth. I lie and tell him I love the role I was hired to play—I love the bambino—and, no, there is no other role in the script that I like (that part is true).

Obviously the producer, poor man, was in a terrible bind. The next day when I suggested a solution he was, to say the least, extremely cooperative. I suggested I play another part—but one that was not in the script. In fact one that was not even written. I created it that morning and described it in detail. He loved it (he had no choice). So it all worked out—the director got his bambino and I got a new part that I felt was terrific—about ten times better than the original. The part had some humor plus a powerful end—my character's sudden unexpected death.

One quick story, and remember this is 1962—the height of the Cold War—the government ran everything—even the film industry. . . .

Once the picture is finished, I am asked to meet the head of all Soviet films. It was the height of the Cold War and the government ran everything. He's sitting on one end of a very long, narrow table, and I'm on the other end. The atmosphere is tense and the head of Soviet films has a neck the size of an automobile tire. He launches into a story about how, on a trip to New York, he made friends with an American on the plane and they made plans to meet for dinner. However, when the American arrived at his hotel, he called the Russian to say that the FBI insisted the dinner plans be canceled. I'm thinking, why is he telling me this story? Number one, it sounds made up, and two, we just met, and now he's slamming the United States. I tell him I had had just the opposite experience in Russia. Everyone was warm and friendly, and if I hadn't been arrested three times it would have been a perfect trip.

That statement was true. People were warm and friendly and I *was* arrested twice. (I threw an extra one in for good measure.) Arrested once for taking a picture of an extraordinary-looking old peasant woman in the marketplace and once for hanging around with a young Russian black marketeer. I got a kick out of that kid. He reminded me of the wise guys who hung out in New York City pool halls. He enjoyed pointing out the secret police working undercover in the hotel lobby. They were supposed to be undercover, but he not only knew who they were, he would chuckle and tell me where they lived and the names of their wives.

Once he knew for sure that I was an American, his eyes lit up. He knew the Italian designers—knew Saks Fifth Avenue. He was savvy in these matters. He figured he could buy from me the latest in men's fashions and resell them for a big profit. I let him come up to my room. He looked at my stuff in the clothes closet. He was immediately disappointed. Nothing interested him, but he did say if I wanted to donate anything to the homeless, he would give me an address. As mentioned earlier, I was never a clotheshorse.

it's a mad, mad, mad, mad world

IF THE CAST OF *Wind Across the Everglades* was eccentric, the cast of *It's A Mad, Mad, Mad, Mad World* was extraordinary. Director Stanley Kramer gathered the top comedians in the business. Get a load of this lineup: Buster Keaton, Milton Berle, Jonathan Winters, Sid Caesar, Buddy Hackett, Mickey Rooney, Phil Silvers, Ethel Merman, Eddie "Rochester" Anderson, Terry Thomas, Edie Adams, and Dick Shawn. There was also Spencer Tracy and, I might add, yours truly.

I played the part of a New York cabdriver who's pulled into the crazy chase. It was only a small part, but that didn't matter, I just wanted to hang around with that bunch of comics.

The following is an attempt to capture the typical day in the making of the picture. Portuguese Bend is a cliff south of Los Angeles overlooking the Pacific Ocean. There was a lull in the activity, the crew was off somewhere lighting, and we actors were relaxing, taking the sun, seated in our folding cloth chairs facing the ocean. We were about 250 feet from the edge of the cliff. Suddenly Milton Berle tapped my elbow and pointed to a spot near the edge of the cliff. I looked and saw a man's arm reaching over the cliff and clutching at the grass in the ground. Then his other arm appeared, pulling his upper body over the cliff. This was an alarming sight, and someone not connected with the movie would have run to give help. But we actors knew better. This was not a man in distress. This was Jonathan Winters—doing what he loved to do— playing a role in some fantasy he was creating. The character we had just seen, who had somehow managed to pull himself up over the cliff, appar- ently had something wrong with his stomach because Jonathan was clutching his abdominal area with one hand while his other hand tore off some grass and applied it to what must have been a bloody wound.

At the sound of an airplane, Jonathan's head jerked up—his hand was now waving a white handkerchief in the air, hoping to get the pilot's attention. Of course, the plane kept going. Then some other people arrived, at least that's what it looked like, because Jonathan was now engaged in an imaginary animated conversation.

By this time, the rest of us actors had gotten up and moved close enough to hear what he was saying. He was talking to an Indian chief, all the while clenching his wound and begging for his life—begging to be forgiven for some unmentionable act involving himself and the chief's beautiful daughter.

He then made reference to a chest of gold which, if someone would be kind enough to remove the spear from his stomach, he could go get, and then present to the Chief as an apology.

As I indicated earlier, this was not an unusual occurrence on this pic- ture. A couple of days earlier, Jonathan was seen making love to a palm tree. His arms were wrapped around the trunk. His head lay against the bark, his eyes closed. His lower body moved rhythmically as he whispered sweet nothings to the tree.

> JONATHAN
> (*To the palm tree*)
> I love you, darling. You're so beautiful—and please don't
> ever—(now Jonathan looked upward toward the top of the
> palm tree)—don't ever change your hairdo.

I also could have just as easily selected almost any day in the back of the truck. The back of the truck—and it was a big truck—was where all

courtesy of Photofest

the comedians congregated. Every day there, they were hanging out in the back of a truck—a dozen of the world's funniest guys doing their thing: stories, jokes, one-liners, songs, and maybe Jonathan remembering something—like the circus night at Madison Square Garden—the farewell address—the final performance of a 102-year-old aerialist—and the introduction of his successor, his eight-month-old grandson Benito—it was a memorable night for the Ringling Brothers and Jonathan did all the sounds—the lion's roar, the squeal of wagon wheels, the crowd's noise, and finally little Benito's gurgle when he was introduced to the crowd. . . . Another usual day on the *Mad, Mad, Mad, Mad World*.

robin and the seven hoods

THE PHONE RANG. It was Frank Sinatra.

I should mention that I hadn't spent much time with Sinatra. A few years earlier, I was in the same elevator with him. Not just me; there were three other people in the elevator, too. He got in on the third floor and out on the sixth. That's how well I knew him.

So when it's him on the phone, I'm a bit off balance—I'm surprised, pleased, and, most of all, curious. Why was he calling me? We exchanged pleasantries. A few lines about a guy that worked for Frank who I had run into recently. Then he said, "I'm making a movie—me and the boys—Dean, Sammy, and Bing—and I want you to be in it. I'll send you a script and you'll let me know."

WOW! What do you know! The crooner himself. That was something! I thought, "Oh, God, I hope there's no conflict." At that time, there was an important part I hoped to play. A strong character, but more importantly, he *was a doctor, not another gangster.* In those days, I was king of the gangster parts. You want a gangster, get Falk. That's all they offered me—one after the other. They were all the same. The only thing that changed was the wardrobe. For an actor, that's a killer. I was in a rut and would never grow, playing the same cliché in every picture. That's why I zeroed in and became focused totally on getting that doctor part; I'd play somebody who had read a book.

But now, hold the phone, folks, Frank's script is coming and I couldn't wait to read it. When it arrived a few days later, I was so excited that I tore open the envelope. The first thing I saw in big black letters was robin and the seven hoods. My heart sank. There was that word, *HOODS*—ANOTHER HOOD! My sails went flat, all the wind gone.

To my surprise, it was a musical. The story centered on Frank's gang—Frank, Dean, Sammy, and Bing. They were hoodlums, mafia outlaws, but they had a decent streak. From what they stole, they were known to toss some in the direction of the needy; hence the name Robin Hood. Everybody had heard of them. They were in all the newspapers. They were riding high. However, they went up my character's rear like a skyrocket. I was to play a big cheese old-fashioned wise guy mob boss. What *my* boys stole, my boys kept. I ran all the mobs in the city—been doing it for years, and I had had enough of this Robin Hood crap.

Sure, it was the role of a gangster, but it was also a very good part. To make matters worse, I had some terrific scenes. But would this bury me deeper? I could hear the town talk—"Did you see Falk in Frank's picture? Terrific!" When you need a "wise guy," it's a no-brainer—get Falk.

I was really torn. I wanted badly to work with the "Rat Pack." It was murder trying to make up my mind. But my whole body said if you get the doctor part, take it—break out of this pigeonhole—do it now before it's too late.

I called Frank. I explained I had a chance to play a doctor, someone unlike any character I had ever played.

PETER

I love your script. I'm sick missing this chance to play with you and the boys, but my instincts tell me if I can play a guy who has a diploma on the wall I'll be better off in the long run.

Is Sinatra great or what? Hear his answer:

FRANK

Do what you think is best for you. You think the doctor—go get it—I wish you luck—but hear this—the part in my picture is yours till the day we start shooting. If for any reason you're available and want in—pick up the phone—I'll send a car.

Can you ask for more? No way.

Friday morning arrived, and I was told another actor had been hired to play the doctor. I yelled to the agent, "Call Sinatra immediately—that means *right now.*"

The deal was closed before lunch. Frank sent the car. I got my wardrobe before dinner, and on Monday the movie started shooting and I was in it. A fairy-tale ending.

What was Frank like as a producer? A quick story will answer that question.

I didn't like a couple of lines I had in a scene coming up. I debated with myself what to do. I knew what I should do—I should talk to the producer. I went looking for Frank. I found him standing next to the coffee pot.

PETER
Frank, I know you're busy, but if you have a moment, I'd like
to speak with you. Is this a good time?

FRANK
Yeah.

PETER (OPENING THE SCRIPT)
I want to show you something. I have it right here, page 29,
my third line, it's—

FRANK (INTERRUPTS)
You don't like what you say? (He rips out the whole page,
throws it on the floor.) Say whatever you want. (And he leaves.)

That's what I call a producer.

Working on that picture was a blast. Off-camera, the boys, as Frank called them, were just like you see them onstage—loose and easy—

plenty of laughs and one big surprise. I didn't notice it when I first read the script. As I mentioned, the movie was a musical and Sammy Caan, the best composer in show business—more hits than Babe Ruth—tapped me on the shoulder. I was bent over inspecting the doughnuts. He told me he wrote a song for me to sing. I was aghast—terrified—I can't sing—can't carry a tune. "Oh *no, no*, Sam, *no* song—*no* singing, *not* me." Later that day, Sinatra summed it up: "You're worried you can't sing? The worse you are, the better it will be." Believe me, folks, I was plenty "worse." Can you imagine? My musical debut—can't carry a tune and singing in a picture with Frank Sinatra, Dean Martin, Sammy Davis, and Bing Crosby.

Me with my daughters Catherine (left) and Jackie.

Ossining, New York, high school. Senior class picnic, June 1945, at Playland, Rye Beach, New York. Seated from left, Doris Heron and Margaret Van Gorp. Standing from left, Eileen Landy, Carolyn Lewis, Barbara Benson, Chickie Ottaviano, Peter, Barbara Kenney, Red Stevens, Barbara McCollum, and Bob Baker.

Peter and Inger Stevens in *The Dick Powell Show*, "The Prince of Tomatoes". Peter's first Emmy win, 1962.

Hirschfeld drawing portraying Peter and Lee Grant in 1971 play, *The Prisoner of Second Avenue*.

Gena Rowlands and Peter in *A Woman Under the Influence*.

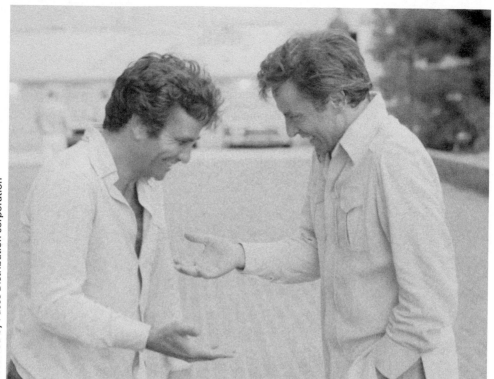

Peter and John Cassavetes share a laugh during the filming of *A Woman Under the Influence*.

Bob Dishy, Peter, Ben Gazzara, and John Cassavetes backstage at *Grown Ups*, a 1981 Broadway play.

Peter with beautiful Faye Dunaway, who guest starred in *Columbo* episode "It's All in the Game."

Columbo director Vince McVeety and Peter.

Penny Peyser, Alan Arkin, and Peter in a scene from his 1979 movie *The In-Laws*.

The Cheap Detective: top, Louise Fletcher and Stockard Channing; middle, Madeline Kahn, Peter, Eileen Brennan; front, Marsha Mason and Ann-Margret.

the great race

I'VE MADE A lot of fun pictures, but *The Great Race* is one of my favorites. Like *It's A Mad, Mad, Mad, Mad World,* *The Great Race* also had a wildly insane premise centering around a car race: only this was a race between two teams—one good, one evil—that begins in Los Angeles and ends in Paris at the Eiffel Tower, of all places. A story that wacky could only come from the comic mind of Blake Edwards. At the time, Blake was known chiefly as the director of now-classic films like *The Pink Panther* and *Breakfast at Tiffany's.* Although I still had not thought of myself as a comedic actor per se—that would come later when working with Neil Simon—I fit the bill for a part in Blake's movie.

The race is between handsome Tony Curtis—dressed in a spotless white suit behind the wheel of his glamorous white convertible— with the breathtakingly beautiful Natalie Wood at his side. Their opponents are a pair of hall-of-fame villains, dressed appropriately head to toe in black: the maniacal Professor Fate played by Jack Lemmon and me in the role of his dumb sidekick Max. Jack was a prince to work with. He only wanted to please people, a lovely man.

The professor's car is designed for any eventuality, including turning into a bicycle built for two that's suspended beneath a hot-air balloon 3,000 feet above sea level. Both men pedal frantically as they battle headwinds, while the professor spies Tony and Natalie's white convertible cruising below through his telescope.

You may ask yourself, "How does a person drive from Los Angeles to Paris?" Easy, when you're ingenious like the professor: you park on a glacier and drift across the Atlantic Ocean. And if the water freezes, it might slow you down, but it will not interfere with dinner. You simply cut a hole in the ice, drop a line, and eat fish.

Keep in mind that this was the early 1960s, and I still saw myself as an off-Broadway theater actor who had stumbled into the Hollywood dreamworld. Just a few years earlier I had been playing 150-seat theaters in Greenwich Village doing Molière, now I found myself in a stage the size of a football field. As if the size of the stage didn't blow my mind, the fact that it was filled entirely with water doubled my amazement—who would even dream of such a thing. Suddenly, I felt like I was a million miles from my New York City acting roots. So this was what a big Hollywood extravaganza looked like. I'd never seen anything like it, but there I was, smack in the middle of it.

Among all this zaniness, here's what people most often recall from the film:

#1. The final scene in Paris as both cars come roaring down the stone steps neck and neck, the crowd screaming, pedestrians fleeing, the cars heading to the Eiffel Tower.

#2. Professor Fate's constant instructions to his copilot, "Push the button, Max."

#3. And the pie fight to end all pie fights—a hundred people throwing a thousand pies—face after face turning and being splashed with a bull's-eye shot to the nose and mouth—and me, Peter, ignoring everyone but Jack and Tony. They were the ones I wanted and when I got them, I got 'em good—three shots in a row, pie crust and applesauce smack in the middle of the face. It was beautiful. Neither one of them ever got me—not once. They tried, oh yeah, they did, but I was too fast for them.

I just remembered something I should mention: my doubt about my playing this part. I never had a part like it. I wasn't sure what it was—sometimes, when I first read it, I felt it resembled something out of vaudeville or a two-man comedy team—Abbott and Costello—it was character comedy intermingled with sight gags—one depending upon the other, but like nothing I had ever done before. I was filled with doubt—anxious—lots of nights staring at the ceiling—finally I just said jump in, it's not cancer. And that's what I did. I jumped. I'm glad I did. The movie turned out to be fun, and a very good film, if I must say so myself.

NOTE TO THE READER

Regarding the next section, there's no common theme. The stories bounce around from one subject to another. The only thing they share is that they're favorites of mine; from a fabulous Arthur Miller story to a tribute to my all-time favorite friend and on to the time I was arrested in Genoa. Happy reading.

arthur miller
tells a good story

THE MOVIE *THE* Misfits had an extraordinary amount of star power. For openers, no film writer was better known than the legendary playwright Arthur Miller, and few couples on the entire planet, obviously, were as well-known as Arthur Miller and Marilyn Monroe. Added to this pair were Clark Gable, Montgomery Clift, and director John Huston. However I was struck by another name that was in that cast: James Barton.

Barton had played the lead in the original Broadway production of *The Iceman Cometh*. Long before that, he had done vaudeville, and after his many years on stage counted Arthur Miller and John Huston among his fans. But Barton was also known as one of the biggest drinkers in show business. Nevertheless, Arthur Miller said that both he and Huston wanted Barton for *The Misfits*. They knew he would be great and could use the money, so they hired him.

Sometime in the middle of shooting the picture, Arthur walked into a saloon and there was James Barton sitting at the bar with a seven-year-old kid. Miller asked, "Who's the kid?" Barton explained that the boy was his grandson and he was taking care of him. Then Barton raised a finger for emphasis, "But you gotta watch this kid every minute; you take your eyes off him for one second and he'll run off to school."

courtesy of Photofest

on what i had
and you didn't—
a lou lilly in my life

IT WOULD BE a wonderful thing if everybody had a "Lou Lilly" in his life. What made Lou so memorable? I guess over a span of 30 years, I'd run into Lou a couple of times a month . . . and practically every time I saw him, he made me laugh. Yes, five out of six times he'd make me laugh—and you know what?—he never told me a joke. There was no one like Lou.

Lou won an Academy Award. He wasn't an actor, but he should have been. Lou created the Bugs Bunny cartoons that we all enjoyed so much. He wrote them and he drew them, and that's how he earned his Oscar.

He also drew this cartoon. I saw it at his house and made him make me a copy.

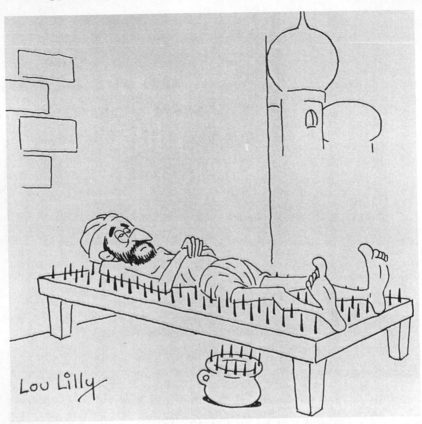

Lou had a lot of child in him—he loved mischief—and the mischief he loved the most was to set me up with some story, reel me in, and watch me fall for it hook, line, and sinker. And every time he got me I'd swear he'd never get me again. But he always did.

We were previewing *The Prisoner of Second Avenue* prior to Broadway. We were in either Boston or Washington, and the stage manager came into my dressing room with the mail. When you're on the road, the bulk of the mail comes from local media, fans, and other people you've never met. But on this day I noticed a special delivery letter that the stage manager said he had signed for. I looked and it was from Lou Lilly. We had never written each other prior to this—and the letter was marked personal and confidential, so naturally I was anxious to open it. But because the stage manager was waiting to speak to me, I excused myself first saying just give me a minute. I turned away and opened Lou's letter. It read:

Kiss my ass
Regards, Lou

Peter, Lou Lilly, and Don Johnson

Another time, I was sitting with the guys in the card room at the golf club. We were arguing sports. Lou pulled up a chair very near our table but not close enough to actually be a part of it. He positioned his chair where he had a clear view of me and he took out a small sketchpad and a pencil and started drawing me. Because Lou made his living drawing animated cartoons, he was very skillful with a pencil. That was an interest we shared: we both liked to draw and talk about it.

From my own experience, I know it's helpful to the artist if the model minimizes the amount of head movement, which I did. Of course, like everyone else, I become self-conscious when a camera is pointed in my direction or someone is drawing me—my mouth tightens—and I can't stop thinking about how I'm going to look. It was only ten or twelve minutes—about right for a quick sketch—when Lou got up, unobtrusively tore the page out, and slipped it under a dessert plate. He nodded to me that he was leaving it for me and left. I didn't want to look like a jerk and rush over, so very casually I eased over and got my drawing. It was placed facedown under the plate; but as soon as I turned it over, I saw:

Kiss my ass
Regards, Lou

It must have been in the early 1990s and Lou was in his late eighties. His golf game was obviously nowhere near what it used to be. Lou had been a helluva player. A single digit handicapper—not long, but from 130 yards in, he was the best in the club. I was standing near the clubhouse watching Lou and his foursome putt out on the 18th green. Lou saw me; we waved to each other. He approached his putt. The ball was practically in the hole and Lou had only to tap it in, which he did, and then to my surprise he shot both arms above his head in triumph. A few minutes later I saw Lou pulling up in his golf cart. His eyes were shining; he was beaming ear-to-ear. I knew what he wanted, and I obliged.

PETER
How did you make out?

LOU

Not too bad, my boy.

PETER

You took everybody's money?

LOU

You got that right.

PETER

What did you shoot?

LOU

84.

PETER

Bullshit.

LOU

No, really—84. I had a helluva round.

PETER

Bullshit.

Lou shrugged his shoulders. He wasn't going to argue. He got a pencil and started putting the final touches on the scorecard. Meanwhile, I got involved in conversation with someone else. But I noticed Lou go into the bag room. Then one of the guys from Lou's foursome, Guy McElwaine, passed me on his way to Lou's cart.

GUY

You shoulda been with us today. That old bastard had a hel-luva round.

PETER

(*chuckling*)

He told me he had 84.

GUY (GOING OVER LOU'S SCORECARD)

He did.

PETER

He did what?

GUY

He had 84.

PETER

Bullshit.

I grabbed the card. There it was—"Kiss my ass. Regards, Lou."

One day I was headed out of the club toward my car in the parking lot when Lou called my name and gestured for me to wait. He had some-thing to tell me. As he approached, he looked rather serious and I wondered what he had on his mind. Here's what was on his mind:

"Peter, if you have a moment, this shouldn't take too long. As you know, Christine and I have been married for 50 years, and naturally we don't have that many conversations that are all that new or provocative. But last night out of the blue, Christine and I had this really interesting talk. She said there was something she wanted to ask me, and I could tell from her manner that she was really interested in my answer.

"What she said was, 'Lou, think about this before you answer: If you had to name just one person in the whole world—aside from me—just one person to be your only friend, who would it be?' I thought for a moment, and I asked: 'Does the person have to be someone I know—someone who has been a part of my life, or can it be someone famous—someone I heard about but I don't know that intimately?' And she said it could be either one—someone you've been close to for many years or someone famous. I thought about that for a while. I wanted to be absolutely honest." (At this point, there was a silent beat as Lou looked directly into my eyes.)

"'So, Christine,' I said, 'I assume from what you said that it would be all right to pick someone from show business.'" (For the first time when he said show business, I thought it might be me—I certainly wasn't sure, but I felt my eyes moisten and if he said my name, I was prepared to wrap my arms around him.) "Christine said, 'Of course it could be someone from show business'—but she stressed that 'The important thing is you only have one pick for one person to be your friend, and you should be thinking substance'—and I told her I had been thinking substance—and I knew who I wanted"—(Lou paused and he again looked straight into my face)—"and I told her it *was* someone in show business and I told her *who*. It was Rin Tin Tin."

For those of you too young to remember, Rin Tin Tin was a famous dog from the movies. Everyone knew him and loved him.

When Lou was in his seventies, his daughters asked him how he wanted them to handle the funeral. Did he want to be buried or cremated? This was not a subject Lou looked forward to discussing, and he avoided answering them. It's six years later, and they still don't know, so they go to him and say they have to know and insist that he tell them. His answer to them was brief—"Surprise me."

getting arrested in genoa

MY GIRLFRIEND SHEILA and I were in Paris. The bloom was off the romance. It was our last night together. We would spend it on a train—the Orient Express, where we had a private compartment. We had prepared a picnic box complete with a fine red wine. She and I boarded in Paris in the evening and would arrive in Genoa the following morning, where we would kiss good-bye and then wave to each other, she on the dock, me at the ship's railing headed for the open seas and a trans-Atlantic crossing back home to New York City.

The wine knocked us out but good. We were on the train, in our compartment, asleep in each other's arms, when suddenly there was a banging on our door. An importunate voice barking out commands in Italian:

VOICE

Italian Customs. Open the door. (bang)

Open the door. Italian Customs. (bang)

SHEILA (ANSWERING IN ITALIAN)

I couldn't be less impressed.

Her snotty response was not too smart, because when we finally opened the door, the customs official made certain that he did a thorough search of our room, turning my suitcase upside down and dumping its entire contents on the bunk. He then left with a very polite "Arrivederci."

However, this "commedia" turned out to be very important—I repeat, very important. It caused me to check the time, and I realized with dread that if we were just now crossing the frontier into Italy, something had gone terribly wrong and I was now in danger of missing my boat.

Sheila made inquiries in Italian. She spoke to the conductor and to other passengers. We found out the boat station was right next to the train station—one small block away—in a taxi it was two minutes. I estimated I had between five and eight minutes to catch the boat before it sailed.

As the train was pulling into the Genoa station, I was already outside the door on the platform—actually on the second step—holding the rail with one hand and my suitcase with the other. It sounds like a bad movie; but as the train slowed to a stop, there was actually a well-groomed, expensively dressed lady with a small dog anxious to be the first to board. I didn't knock her down, but I rocked her backward as I tore off that train and headed full bore toward the exits. I could see the doors and the ticket-taker in front of them. I was moving in his direction.

I held my suitcase not by the handle, but tucked under my armpit—nothing banging against my legs. I had been on the track team in high school. I was nothing special; but for one year, I was the best half-miler we had. So when the ticket-taker asked for my passport and ticket, I didn't miss a step. I went past him like a blur headed for a taxi. I could still hear him yelling "passaporto, biglietto." I turned. He was chasing me. As the taxi pulled out, I looked back again.

Now there were two guys chasing me, both yelling "passaporto, biglietto." Meanwhile I was yelling at the cabdriver, "Nave, nave" [ship, ship], all the while dumping whatever Italian money I had into his lap. He floored the gas pedal and was laughing as we roared past a little guardhouse with the guard standing out front, both hands raised indicating we should stop. Now there were three guys chasing us, all yelling "passaporto, biglietto."

We picked up a fourth as we ignored the guard stationed at the entrance to the grounds of the boat station. He was slow and fat, but behind him the other three guys from the other station came into view, and all three were still charging and yelling for the passport.

I was now in the boat building looking around wildly, not knowing where to go. Then I saw the sign "embarca," with an arrow pointing down. I hit those stairs hard—nearly killed myself going down them. At the bottom, I pushed through two swinging doors and then came to an abrupt stop. I was suddenly outdoors.

I was on the dock, and raising up beside me, like a gigantic whale, was the huge black hull of the ship. It hadn't sailed. I had made it. I was so relieved, so happy. Then the thought—how do I get on? I heard loud voices. I looked down the dock. Oh, my lord—they were pulling up the gangplank. An official on the dock was yelling instructions to sailors on the ship.

I started running toward the official—running and yelling. From a distance, he noticed me coming, but he was still occupied with the gangplank. I of course kept running and yelling and pointing at the ship. When I finally got closer to him, still shouting and making faces, he raised his arms and gestured to me to calm down. He then put out his hand and said "Passaporto. Biglietto." I was stunned. For a second there was just stillness. I was trying to control myself. I took a deep breath and forced my rage backward—down and backward, from whence it came into my throat.

With an outward calm I placed my suitcase on the dock and, moving deliberately so I wouldn't explode, I lowered myself to one knee, flipped the latch, and opened the top. I knew my passport was under my socks on the left side near the rear and my ticket was to the right of my passport. How stupid of me. I should have had them in my pocket. As I reached for them, I heard a rumble. Still on one knee, I glanced up and saw that the hull was moving—very slowly—but moving. Looking higher, I realized the entire ship was moving. There was a blast from the ship's horn, and then I knew that this ship was never going to stop. It was on its way. And with that in mind, and with one continuous swift motion, I brought my passport and ticket up and out of the suitcase and slapped them across the official's face.

This naturally started a fight. He swung and I swung—we both half landed—he grabbed and I grabbed—for a moment it was a half-assed standoff, and then suddenly I was hurled to the ground, guys sitting on both arms and legs. It felt like an army on top of me, but actually it was only three guys—the same three who had been chasing me. They were getting in their licks, but in the confusion I could make out someone beating down on them: Sheila was cracking them over their heads with an umbrella.

The whole thing ended with the arrival of the police and me in the clink.

I suppose there are some people who would argue that I got what I deserved. Having to show a passport is the law—not only in Italy, but throughout the world, including the United States.

They put me in a cell and let me cool my heels for about three hours. I was then taken to the office of the police chief. Sheila was already in the room, but we weren't allowed to talk to each other. The chief was a big man about the size of a Buick. From the shape of his nose, he had either walked into a lot of doors or was an ex-heavyweight. Either way, if you wanted to give somebody lip, you wouldn't pick him.

He didn't waste time using an old expression. He let it be known that he had in one hand a carrot and in the other a stick, which hand he would use was up to me. I had been disrespectful of the law and the men hired to enforce it. He wanted an apology. He looked at me, then at his watch and said, "It's up to you—the carrot or the stick. Make up your mind—apologize—yes or no!"

I didn't know what the stick was. The chief never said, but I didn't try to find out. I figured, don't take any chances screwing around with that, just start apologizing. As for the carrot, I couldn't care less. I started my apology. I got out about four words when the chief cut me off and yelled to someone in the anteroom.

The door opened and one of the men from the train station who had chased me yelling "passaporto" entered the room.

The chief introduced him—said his full name, said he'd worked that job 12 years, said he was married with four children. Then he told me to start the apology again.

Having to talk directly to this very likeable, decent man affected what I said and the tone with which I said it. I was more genuine. It occurred to me for the first time that the chief may have had a point. When I finished, the chief said, "Now apologize to me." That rubbed me the wrong way, so I'm sure my words of apology were coated with insincerity. When I finished, the chief looked at his guys in the room and started to chuckle. He liked that I showed a little spunk. He seemed to get a kick out of it. This chief was a piece of work. He then told me that the boat that I had seen sail out of Genoa would stop overnight in Naples, and I would have plenty of time to get there and board it tomorrow before it set sail for New York.

As a kid, I never liked carrots, but then before this I never got one from an Italian police chief.

the raisin story

PAUL SHYRE WAS an off-Broadway producer. He was also a finicky eater. One day at the Stage Delicatessen, he couldn't make up his mind what to order and the waiter was getting impatient. Finally Paul decided on rice pudding. As the waiter was writing the order down, Paul interrupted him and said, "Wait a minute. Does the rice pudding have raisins?"

"No."

". . . 'Cause I don't want any raisins."

"There are no raisins."

"Okay, I'll have it. No raisins."

When the rice pudding arrived, Paul looked at it and saw that there were raisins. Paul to the waiter: "There are raisins! I said no raisins."

The waiter, leaving: "Here and there you'll find a raisin."

anzio

IN **1968 I** was offered a role in a movie titled *Anzio*. The film was based on an account of the famous American invasion of Italy in World War II and would be shot overseas. The script had not yet been completed, so my agent and I asked to meet with the writer, who would fill us in on my part.

We met at the Beverly Hills Hotel, where I found myself charmed immediately by the writer's foreign accent. I'm a sucker for foreign accents. However, my enthusiasm was short-lived. I may have enjoyed his lilt, but my part sounded silly. We turned it down. Case closed.

Fast-forward six months. The director, a well-known highly regarded professional, called my agent to say that my part had been completely rewritten. Further, they were prepared to make a huge jump in the amount of dough to play the part. And get this: I would share above-the-title billing with Robert Mitchum. The agent told me to grab it, and so I did. Who could resist top billing? That impressed me more than the money.

I arrived in Rome late at night. Long trip—L.A. to New York, across the ocean to Rome. I was beat. There was a rewritten script at the hotel. I was very anxious to see what it was like. I lay down and began to read it. It wasn't interesting. The characters were all clichés. I fell asleep. The next morning the first thing I checked was the script. My reaction the second time reading it was the same as the first—my part was lousy—"old hat"—nothing to act.

I met with the director, who was delighted to see me. He gave me a big bear hug. I wasted no time, telling him right off that the script was dumb and I was going home. He was understandably taken aback. I called my agent and told him the same thing. He couldn't believe it. The agent suddenly became very nervous. "Have you told Dino? You must see Dino!!"

Oh God, Dino. He was referring to Dino De Laurentiis, arguably the most famous movie producer in the world—made countless pictures—everywhere—in many countries, owned a studio in Rome. He was an awesome force.

When we walked into his enormous office he leapt out of his chair. He was a man with boundless energy, a booming voice, and extravagant gestures. He rushed to greet me, arms wide. "Pee-tur—buon giorno—attore Americano—grande."

"I'm going home," I said.

Dino, smiling, turned to the translator, "What did he say?" The translator told him and Dino roared, clapped his hands, and called me a comedian. He just didn't understand. That I would be going home was unimaginable. Finally, between the agent and the translator, they got through to him. He realized that I was actually booked on a 1:00 p.m. flight to New York. He was stunned into silence. He walked slowly, silently, to his desk, sat down, hung up, still silent, stared out the window, then suddenly slapped the desk, stood up, and said, "I'll drive you to the airport."

We were in Dino's limousine, headed to the airport. Dino sat in the front seat next to the chauffeur. I was in the back with the translator. No one spoke. Dino was too engrossed in the script. The silence was broken only by the sound of Dino turning the pages of the script. After a few minutes of this, he slammed the script shut and said in broken English, "Good. Tell Pee-tur no prob-lema—all good. No prob-lema."

He then explained to the translator something about combining actor A's part with actor C's part, leaving actor C, who was terrific, to play my part—and I should know everything fine—no problema.

I told the translator to tell Dino I was relieved to hear that—happy to know that Dino felt everything fine—no problema.

This exchange was followed by some minutes of silence. Then Dino said to the translator, "Tell Pee-tur when he go back Hollywood I don't want him say bad things about script."

I said, "I would never do that. I'll say it was a terrific script."

Dino nodded, muttered "Good."

A few more minutes and Dino asked, "What will Pee-tur say Hollywood? What reason he no do movie?"

I said, "I'll tell people I got sick on the plane on the way over and it got worse the next day and I just wanted to get home to my doctor."

I could hear some more mutterings. At that moment, we passed a sign announcing the airport. "Stop the car," Dino ordered. He turned around in his seat, his eyes leveling with mine. "WHAT DO YOU WANT?" he bellowed.

What do I want?! What a question! Like this is some poker game and I'm holding a full house. What I want is simple. I want a better part. That's it. Nothing else. And that's what I told him.

"You know a writer?" Dino asked.

My mouth opened, but nothing came out. I was nonplussed for a

Peter as U.S. Army Corporal in "Anzio"

second, then just blurted out the truth: "I don't need a writer. I'll write it myself."

Life is full of surprises. I never in my wildest dreams expected what happened next. Dino extended his right hand. He wanted to shake my hand. When I realized what was happening, I grabbed it. We shook. We made a deal and then drove to the airport and canceled my plane reservation.

I really loved my rewrites for the first two scenes. First scene—it's the night before the invasion. I'm a GI, and my company is scheduled to board a ship at midnight, head north for three hours, then gear up, helmets on, weapons loaded, down the ladder to the landing boats, then wait, crouched on heels, for dawn's early light. At its first glimmer, it happens—10,000 strong hit the beach at Anzio. The first Allied boots on the continent of Europe since 1940—four long years.

My rewritten scene begins around 11 o'clock, an hour before boarding. I'm in the back of a truck—a big comfortable space with a roof. I'm there with three young Italian girls—two of them whores, the third just a friend—but all three are gorgeous. We have wine, and we're all feeling good. There's a soft breeze, and I'm teaching the girls to sing "Bye-Bye Blackbird." They loved saying the words in broken English. We were lying on one another, enjoying each other, laughing and softly singing.

The girls brought salami sandwiches and Italian cheese. They wanted to spend the night in the truck. I told them it's not possible—the army needs the truck at midnight. Then, kissing each girl, slipping them money, the scene ends with my saying, "Tomorrow night we find another truck and a new song." The next shot, I'm boarding the ship heading for the invasion.

Anzio is not my best example of good acting. While I enjoyed my time in Italy, I felt that my career was no longer presenting me with acting challenges. The parts I had played in *It's a Mad, Mad, Mad, Mad World*, *Robin and the Seven Hoods*, and *The Great Race* were lots of fun, but, like my role in *Anzio*, they weren't exactly career-builders. I felt stalled, and I wasn't sure if I'd ever break out of what felt increasingly like a rut. I'd been in films for nearly a decade, and the parts simply weren't coming the way I'd hoped. I was working steadily, but hardly creatively. I was on the verge of being typecast. Although I'm not one to despair, I had begun to have serious doubts about the direction I was headed. Those feelings, however, didn't last long. Along came a police lieutenant named Columbo, and my life would never be the same.

how did the columbo character evolve?

THAT'S A GOOD question. Where did I begin? Before we ever started shooting, what were my earliest thoughts? I was struck very early on by the dramatic possibilities of playing a man who housed within himself two opposite traits. On the one hand being a regular Joe, the guy next door, nothing special, and at the same time being the most brilliant detective on the globe. A guy with a mind like Einstein who sounded like the box boy at Food Giant.

In life I, Peter Falk, sound like a street kid. In life I dress like a slob, so I knew I was going to enjoy the ordinary side of Columbo since being ordinary comes easy for me. On the other hand, I'm also odd like the lieutenant. My mind is off someplace. Where? Frequently it's on a script—more specifically, on my character in the script; what my character does, thinks, says. If any of it strikes me as false, or boring, I get obsessed with making the character more interesting or amusing—something—anything to keep the audience involved.

Now Columbo is known for other traits. He has an obsessive insistence that minutia be measured accurately. This is something he got from me, and in this area I can say I'm his superior. For example, when I weigh myself in order to get an accurate measurement, it is not enough for me to remove all my clothes including my socks—I also remove my watch and my one contact lens—just kidding.

So it was easy for me to spot another obsessive like Columbo. At first blush he appears likeable, easygoing, nonthreatening; but for me, Peter, I saw a part of Columbo that was like part of me. I saw a man who had an obsessive streak. I saw that behind the raincoat was someone who couldn't sleep until he found the answer.

Faye Dunaway, in a script written by yours truly, asked Columbo what's the longest he's ever worked on a case. He answered 11 years. It took 132 months, but finally it was over. He found the answer.

When you think of a homicide detective, you don't think of an absentminded professor. However, Columbo is not your average detective. Take the astronomer obsessed by the big questions: How did the universe begin? What caused the Big Bang? This is a man who can understandably forget where he put his car keys. Columbo is no different.

For him, the questions presented at the murder scene are equally consuming. They possess him—anything else gets lost. It's no wonder that when he reaches into his raincoat pocket for a damning piece of evidence, he comes out instead with a piece of paper—a written reminder, e.g., a quart of milk and a dozen eggs.

I don't remember the exact episode when I first put one of those written reminders in my raincoat pocket, but when I took it out I sure remember it taking the murderer by surprise. Oh, the look on that actor's face. There he was, gearing up for a defense against a damning bit of evidence, and out of Columbo's pocket came . . . "a loaf of bread and a box of raisins." You could read the murderer's thoughts: "I was right from the beginning. This Columbo can't be a cop—he's too dumb."

You can imagine how all those fantastic actors who came aboard the show enjoyed these unplanned, spontaneous moments. For actors, surprises are delicious. We love them.

Columbo's absentmindedness was right up there at the top of the things that I love most about him. Every chance I got, I'd try to bum a match, ask someone if they had an extra pencil, pat my pockets trying to locate the one where I put my notebook. These were the mannerisms that evolved and soon made up the Columbo character.

Another thing I realized about him—appearing intelligent made him uneasy—it put him at a disadvantage. He was much more comfortable looking a bit slow—it was relaxing for him to give the impression of mediocrity. He knew he had you where he wanted you. That's why whenever he had a brilliant insight, it was fun to rework the scene and assign the idea to one of his relatives—attribute the observation to his brother-in-law or an egghead nephew. You've never seen a detective with so many brothers-in-law or a larger army of relatives, all coming up with brilliant ideas.

Here's a sampling of folks he's mentioned: a sister who likes modern furniture, a nephew who wears contact lenses, a brother who's 38 and still has his high school sneakers, a father-in-law who loves western movies, a brother-in-law who's a waiter, a brother-in-law named George, a brother-in-law in the National Guard, an uncle who played bagpipes with the Shriners, a cousin in Albany who wears thick glasses and plays chess, a nephew majoring in dermatology at UCLA, an uncle who drove a bus until he made a killing in real estate, a cousin and brother-in-law who run an auto body shop in the valley, nieces who like rock music, a sister-in-law who drinks, a nephew who is a champion weightlifter and needlepointer, a nephew who wants to be an accountant, a teenage nephew who wants to be a director, and a mother-in-law in Fresno.

How does the raincoat fit into all of this? What I remember vividly is just a few days before shooting the first episode, Columbo's wardrobe was laid out on a huge bed. There were the usual suits and coats—light and dark—summer and winter—there was even a short driving coat—sweaters, shirts, ties. Immediately I felt disappointed. These clothes could have been worn by thousands of men from all walks of life. There was nothing distinctive. Nothing to remember.

What do I mean by that? Well, take Charlie Chaplin's costume. We remember that, don't we—the derby and the cane? How about Art Carney's character on *The Honeymooners*—that vest and hat. I don't know when the raincoat in my upstairs closet popped into my mind and I don't know why it popped into my mind. It was just instinct. Working from the seat of my pants. I couldn't explain it. I asked a wardrobe person to take one of the suits—a blue-and-white summer seersucker suit—and dye it a drab brown. I wanted it to match my raincoat. Then I was on a roll. A pair of my shoes came to my mind as well. Brown shoes that I had bought in Italy that had a high back that came way up above the ankle and looked like something an immigrant might wear. Then I added a drab green tie that I had had for a thousand years.

The whole costume was assembled in a couple of days. I looked in the mirror and loved what I saw. In fact, I liked it so much that I decided there would be no second coat—no second suit—no change of clothes at all. Columbo doesn't need an entire wardrobe—just what I had on did the trick. *That's it!* Nothing else but what's in the mirror.

Now came the questions from both the network and the studio. Why does a man wear a raincoat in sunny California? Suppose he has to go to the beach. Does he wear a raincoat on the beach? Why does a man have only one suit? He wears the same thing every day—365 days a year!

These were of course reasonable questions. But I must say the opposition wasn't adamant. The studio and network executives were uneasy about it, but at the end of the day they said, "If that's what he wants, we'll live with it." It was also cheap—that's always a plus.

How does the car fit into all of this? I remember that the day before we were scheduled to start shooting, Bill Link and Dick Levinson, the executive producers, yelled out the window, "We've just scheduled a scene for tomorrow's shoot that requires Columbo's car. Go down to the garage and pick something you like."

That Columbo needed a car never occurred to me. Cops in my mind drove police cars. Who knew or even would think to ask what a homicide detective drives? Anyway, I went down to the garage and there were hundreds of cars and, as with the wardrobe, none of them grabbed me. None said anything about their owners. I wanted something distinctive.

Leaving the garage, I turned for a final look. And there it was, nose peeking out from the back wall. A beat-up, weathered gray, one-of-a-kind convertible. And talk about the perfect touch—it had a flat tire. I knew that was it. *It even matched the raincoat.*

Coming up with the raincoat and car just a day or two before shooting began was an unexpected blessing. These two additions were big— giant advances in the development of the Lieutenant. We got off to a helluva start.

The next thing that developed was Columbo's exquisite politeness. And this happened in the very first episode. I called all men "Sir" and all women "Ma'am." I sprinkled "No, sirs" and "Yes, ma'ams" and "I beg

Columbo with his Peugeot

your pardons" all over the room. And once again, that was gut instinct. If you ask me why, I couldn't explain it. In hindsight, I often said that Columbo was by nature a polite man from birth. Being polite was not an act, and I believe that. However, in that first episode it just happened. It came out for no conscious reason. It just felt right, and it continued to feel right for 30 years.

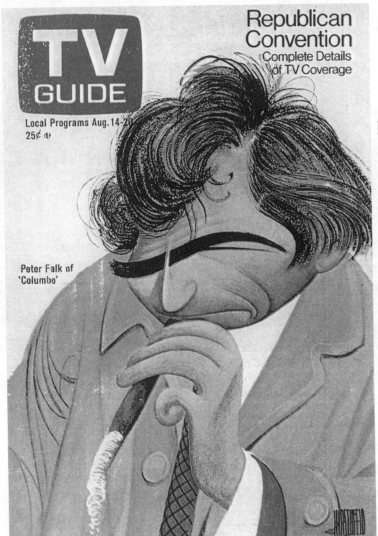

Al Hirschfeld's drawing of Columbo for *TV Guide* Cover

columbo odds and ends—to play columbo—makeup not required—unlike some other actors

AFTER THE RAINCOAT and the car, the next step—*"the Columbo look."* That was easy, only one requirement: *look bad. No makeup.* People would say "You forgot to shave"—Good! "You need a haircut." Good! Now everything, the car, the coat, and my face, all matched.

Hirschfeld nailed it. He is fantastic—what an *artist.* Look at that drawing—is that great, or what?!

Columbo also had a dog. The problem with having a dog on a TV series is the dog's age. We got the first dog in 1971 and he was already very old. He passed in '73, and his replacement was much younger. This caused a problem.

I was in and out of makeup in no time, I was ready very fast but we couldn't shoot. Had to wait for the dog. Where was he? He was in makeup. That's right—sitting in the barber's chair—munching dog bones—while the makeup girls, his fans, using a powder puff, would apply clown white to his face to make him look older. Thirty minutes shot to hell.

"this old man, he played one— he played knickknack on my thumb"

FROM AS FAR back as I can remember, that bouncy, funny, infectious little tune with those droll lyrics always tickled me. The next verse—get this! "This old man, he played two, he played knickknack on my shoe. . . ." No idea what any of it means. I just chuckle.

At any rate, that tune was introduced on Columbo in a 1973 episode starring Donald Pleasence and Julie Harris. Introduced in such a tiny way, you could hardly hear Columbo humming it. Over the passage of time, it's hard to believe, but this odd little tune became the Columbo theme song, soaring as, at times, thirty musicians and a conductor turned it into a full-blown orchestral symphony.

Let me go back to the beginning. The first time the tune was used was in a small uneventful scene in the basement of a building. Columbo was alone using a wall phone to call the newspaper to get

Julie Harris, Peter, and Donald Pleasance in a 1973 *Columbo* episode

the weather conditions in a beach area on a certain day in the previous week. The voice at the newspaper told Columbo, "Please be patient. This will take a few minutes. I have to look up the information." The scene continued. That is, the camera kept running as I waited, holding the phone. Very quickly I became aware of the big bad camera five feet away pointed at my face. I didn't know what to do. Just standing there mute holding a phone to my ear is not that compelling. I became increasingly self-conscious. Then I heard myself humming and then, looking for some variety, heard myself actually singing "knickknack paddy whack," but very quietly, because I can't sing and I didn't want people to know that. Hard to believe, but that moment was the birth of the Columbo theme song. Hard to believe, but that's how it all started—me standing there holding the phone and starting to sing because I didn't know what else to do.

So in terms of the Columbo character, what do we have with this tune—this "knickknack paddy whack" song? Why did it catch on? Why was it appropriate? I don't have a fancy answer. It appealed to millions of viewers for the same reason it appealed to me—it's delicious, catchy, and fun. It's appropriate because Columbo should have a favorite tune that's distinctive—that's peculiar to one man and, like the car and the raincoat, separates him from the herd.

columbo odds and ends— god never designed any one human to be recognized by two billion other humans

I COULD BE in a very cold freezing place, nothing but ice and snow, the wind howling, and if from around the corner 200 feet away four Eskimos saw me coming, their eyes would moisten up from happiness at the sight of me (not me, Columbo).

In fact, something along these lines once happened in Ecuador. I was shooting *Vibes* there with Cyndi Lauper and Jeff Goldblum. The cast and crew were driven to the base camp way up in the Andes on the second day. From there, we were loaded into a rickety old bus that took us on a narrow winding dirt road to our location— a small Incan Indian village. After a considerable length of time, we were thousands of feet above sea level when the old bus finally lurched to a stop. Outside, there was one lonely bench placed in a public square. I got out of the bus and headed for the bench when I noticed a bunch of Incan Indian children running toward me, waving their arms and yelling. Even though the language was Spanish, I could make out the words "Columbo! Columbo!—Tenanté Columbo!"

Naturally I was beaming, exhilarated with surprise and delight. It was a kick seeing the excitement and laughter in their faces. I was amazed—in the middle of nowhere, how did they know Columbo? But it didn't take long to notice that even the smallest hut had a TV antenna.

Peter with Equadorian children

columbo
odds and ends—
descriptions

THERE HAVE BEEN many descriptions of Columbo.
My favorite is: Columbo is an ass-backward Sherlock
Holmes.*

The above is perfect just as it is. But I'm a hog and can't help
adding to it. . . .

★ Holmes has a long thin neck—Columbo has no neck.

★ Holmes speaks the King's English—Columbo is still working
on his.

★ Holmes wears tailor-made British tweeds—Columbo's coat
should be cleaned and burned.

★ Oh, another good description—Being chased by Columbo is
like being nibbled to death by a duck.**

---

* Courtesy of Elaine May.

** Courtesy of Jack Horger's son.

what's the toughest thing about creating a columbo?

WHAT'S THE TOUGHEST thing about creating an episode of *Columbo*? What's the mountain that almost every show has to climb?

Think about it this way: In a good murder mystery, there's a murder and there are say five suspects and the audience is glued to the set trying to guess which one of the five did it. The author knows his audience will be there right to the end. The viewer waits to see who did it.

However, in a *Columbo,* you know who the murderer is in the first five minutes. You know how he did it in the first ten minutes. What are you hanging around for? Just one thing: you want to know how he gets caught. But for that, you have to wait another hundred minutes. Now, if someone is watching the tube for one hour and 40 minutes, what they find out better be pretty gosh damn interesting, delightfully unexpected, brilliant, and believable. In short, a terrific scene that's fun to watch. Finding that scene—*finding the clue that's the heart of that scene*—that's the toughest thing about creating a *Columbo*.

You'd be surprised to find out where some of the best clues come from. How about a dentist office? This was a new dentist, I should point out. We never met before. The appointment was for two o'clock and I got there at two. That's because I still believed in miracles. It could happen. It's not likely, but it's possible that if the appointment is for two, the dentist might be ready to see you at two. He wasn't, and I picked up some magazines, looking to pass the time. I browsed through the usual standbys—*Newsweek, Good Housekeeping*—when my eye landed on *Police Chief* magazine. I was curious, picked it up, and saw an article entitled "Bite Mark Evidence."

Well, it turns out that in Fresno, California, in a drug-related murder, a suspect was convicted on the basis of his bite mark left by his teeth on a piece of gum found at the scene of the crime. What a terrific clue for Columbo. My heart beat faster. My mind fixated on a single thought. How was I going to get this magazine out of the dentist's office?

I could conceal it under my shirt and walk out with it immediately. However, the receptionist had a good view of the entire waiting room. I would have to do the actual concealing in the men's room. Talking about the receptionist . . . round about this time, she told me the doctor had finished with the previous patient and would see me in a minute. That eliminated the possibility of walking out with the magazine then and there.

The next decision was whether to go to the men's room now and conceal the magazine, or wait until after my dental work and do it then. I wasn't comfortable with the thought of sitting in the dentist's chair and having this new dentist work on me with the stolen magazine under my shirt. I decided to wait and do the deed on my way out. And that's what I did, I left with the magazine stuffed in my pants.

I then went to my office and put the magazine in my right-hand top desk drawer for safekeeping. I knew one day it would come in handy. Some years later, maybe five, we got a *Columbo* script titled "Agenda for Murder" that had a very good story, but a weak last scene. It was a political story. The two staff writers and the producers were against doing it. They felt politics had very little audience appeal. That fact, plus a very weak ending for which they had no solution, was the basis for their objection.

I disagreed. I took the magazine out of the top desk drawer and sent it along with the script of "Agenda for Murder" to a man who I considered the most underrated, underappreciated talent out there. The first two times that he appeared on *Columbo*, he won an Emmy for "Best Performance by a Guest Star in a TV Series." No other actor in the history of television has had that honor. The Columbo franchise, myself, Universal Studios, and the NBC network—we all are indebted to Patrick McGoohan for his huge contributions to the show. He did everything. He wrote, directed, acted and he did them all brilliantly. He single-handedly lifted the show to new heights.

Pat loved the bite-mark evidence clue. We knew that it would give us a knock-your-socks-off, smashing final scene. Pat agreed to play the murderer, he agreed to direct; and as for rewriting, that came with the territory . . . he did that automatically.

The murderer was a hugely successful brilliant lawyer/politician who was the law partner and the chief of staff for the man just selected to be the candidate for the office of vice president of the United States. Pat decided to make his character a nibbler. He snacks on Life Savers, gum drops, anything—and the night he shoots a racketeer who's threatening to blackmail him, he had nibbled on a piece of cheese that had been put out for visitors. So in the opening investigation scene, the dead

Patrick McGoohan

man is found slumped over his desk, his arm dangling toward the floor, and just beneath his hand on the carpet are the pistol that fired the shot and tiny drops of blood. It was clearly a case of suicide. The dead man was facing a 20-year jail sentence for racketeering. The detective on the scene is briefing Columbo on what has happened. The detective looks up from his notebook and is surprised that Columbo has disappeared. He was standing very visible by the desk beside the dead body, and now he's gone. Actually, he's not gone—he just can't be seen under the desk on his hands and knees inspecting the carpet where the gun and blood drops are located. However, he gets a whiff of something and, following the scent like a hound dog, discovers a piece of Italian cheese on a small plate on the desktop. He holds the cheese up to his nose. He's in heaven. The aroma brings him back to his childhood. This was his father's favorite cheese—Tallego. He insists the detective taste it. The cop declines: "It's evidence. It shouldn't be touched."

Columbo can't resist. A little taste—who will know. And sure enough, he cuts off a piece and savors it. However, what remains has a bite mark in it. What a lovely way to introduce to the 15 million viewers the evidence that an hour later will nail the killer.

So there's no telling where, when, or how we've found these golden clues. In this case, who would have guessed it would be sitting there in my dentist's waiting room?

And, get this, who would have guessed that several years later when we shot this show ("Agenda for Murder"), that same exact magazine from the dentist's office would be in Columbo's pocket in every scene of the movie. That's right—I shoved that sucker into my back pants pocket and kept it there the entire show. The Lieutenant only took it out once. In the final scene, he whips out the magazine and reads it to the murderer. The same lines I had read in the dentist's office five years before were put in the script.

COLUMBO

(to the murderer as he unrolls his magazine)

Did you ever see this? (Points to the magazine title):
Police Chief's magazine. August issue. There's an article in
here—that's how I know about this. (Opens it.)
I found out that in Fresno—a forensic dentist, his name was
Benoff—I'll read it to you—it says he "punctured the alibi of
a suspect in a drug-related slaying by matching a wad of
chewing gum discarded at the scene, to the suspect's teeth.
Seeing the matched models, the suspect pleaded guilty."
This is getting to be a big thing—bite-mark evidence.
That famous serial murderer in Florida. Bundy. He was put
to death on the basis of matching up his teeth to the bite
marks on the bodies of the two girls. This is getting to be big.
I'm glad I read that article.

I might be wearing the raincoat when I said that, but the fact is that's
me, Peter Falk, saying I'm glad I read that article. So the bottom line is,
if I'd had a different dentist, that episode would never have been made.
You just never know where a fantastic clue will turn up next.

great clues

LET'S TALK ABOUT my waking hours during the past thirty years since *Columbo* began. I claim that a significant portion of those hours were spent trying to discover some way to find really good clues. Let me give you an example. Richard Carradine, a member of the famous Carradine family, was a very bright college student and because his mother and my wife were friends, the *Columbo* show was fortunate enough to have the benefit of his services. In short, we got lucky. Richard's job was to come up with clues, read everything in sight—short stories, novels, magazine pieces, court trials, forensic materials. Here's a good one he came up with.

There are candy machines that take coins. Put in a coin, and out comes the candy. They empty the coins from this machine every day and take them someplace to be counted. Go to that place, inspect the coins, and if you find the suspect's fingerprint on one of the coins, you know one thing for certain: between the hours of 1:00 p.m. and 5:00 p.m., he was standing on this street—on this spot in front of the candy machine. How do you know? You know because they empty the coins every four hours starting at 1:00 p.m. So if his fingerprint is found in that batch of coins that were emptied at 5:00 p.m., he was there some time between 1:00 p.m. and 5:00 p.m.

Unfortunately, we couldn't use a candy machine in our script. The murder took place in an apartment on a typical street—no candy machines. But guess what? There were parking meters. How lucky is that? They're just as good. Let's say they empty the parking meters every four hours starting at 1:00 p.m. Now the suspect claims he spent the afternoon in San Bernardino in his girlfriend's apartment making love in his girlfriend's bed. And his girlfriend confirms that. She says he got there around noon. They had a bite to eat and around 2:00 p.m. they got under the covers and stayed there the rest of the day until 6:30 p.m.

We know that can't be true, because sometime between 1:00 and 5:00 p.m. he was not in bed with his girl; he was 30 miles away on this street in downtown Los Angeles and he put a coin in a parking meter.

I like that clue. It's worthy of Columbo—to think of checking the coins in the parking meters for fingerprints—that's brilliant. That's the work of a hall-of-fame homicide detective.

I remember another time when Richard came up with an even more intriguing clue. Listen to this one. It has to do with the way men put on their pants. There are two groups of men: right-handed men and left-handed men. Right-handed men put on their pants one way and left-handed men put on their pants a second way. Right-handers put all their weight on their right leg. They actually stand on their right leg while lifting their left leg and inserting it in the hole provided by the left side of the pants. Left-handers do the opposite. They put all their weight on their left leg—actually stand on it while lifting their right leg and inserting *that* leg in the hole provided by the right side of the pants.

I got very excited. This is a clue that would immediately grab everybody's interest. Who would dream that the world's men are divided into two groups—each group with its own particular way of putting on their pants. It's not only intriguing, it's funny. *But* here's the problem: it sounded fishy. I wanted to believe it, but I didn't. I was skeptical. I didn't know what to do. Then it came to me. I have to test it—YES—I'll conduct my own research. I'll select a subject (Chris Seiter, the *Columbo* show's producer, popped into mind). I'll ask him to do certain things and we'll see what he does. Obviously I can't explain to him what I'm doing—that this is research. This has to be a pure experiment. The subject, in this case Chris Seiter, can't know he's being tested. He has to react instinctively. I figure I'll call him up, ask him to drop his pants and take it from there.

PETER
(*on phone to Chris Seiter*)
Hello, Chris? Peter. . . . I'm going to ask you to do something.
Don't ask any questions. Just do it.

CHRIS
What are you going to ask me to do?

PETER
You're already asking questions. No questions.
Just do what I ask.

CHRIS
But you didn't ask yet.
Before you ask, can't I ask what you're going to ask?

PETER

Just shut up. Okay, here we go.

We're starting now—drop your pants.

(Silence. A beat.)

CHRIS

I'm not asking anything—just confirming. You said,

"Drop your pants?" At least that's what I heard. I heard

"Drop your pants. . . ."

PETER

(*interrupting*)

Are you at your desk?

CHRIS

Yes.

PETER

You're seated?

CHRIS

Yes.

PETER

Well, stand up. You up?

CHRIS

Yes.

PETER

Okay. Walk around the desk and stand in front of it. Let me
know when you're there.

CHRIS

I'm there.

PETER

You're there! Okay, good. You got plenty of room.
Okay, drop your pants.

I'm not going to recount every step. Chris was very slow. It will take
a year. However, he confirmed the theory. He was right-handed and he
stood on his right leg and the left leg went into the pants first.

The next person tested, our director Vince McEveety, was at home
in the living room with his family when I called. He went to his bedroom for the test. However, his test did not support the theory. He was
right-handed and he stood on his left leg.

This process of testing one man at a time was too slow. The next step,
which would be faster, was to bring in a bunch of male tour guides to
a sound stage. Bring in 25 at a clip, lock the door, and have them drop
their pants and then pick them up and put them on. You can imagine
the looks on their faces. I can't begin to describe these sessions—how
hilarious, how interesting, how alive they were. However, we only had
to test two batches of guides. That was enough, the theory was non-
sense. In fact a lot of men vary—sometimes stand on their right, other
times on their left. So much for the pants clue.

Getting genuinely clever clues is tough, mighty tough. Most mys-
teries in both TV and films settle for fake clues—smoke and mirrors.
The audience gets the outer appearance of substance, but they've been

had by a clever director. Believe me, the real babies, like hen's teeth, are hard to find and somebody—some crazy person must insist, no matter what, on finding them.

Talking about how crazy I was rings a bell—brings to mind the early days of *Columbo*. The fights between myself and the studio—the disputes between myself and the producers—the battles. READ ALL ABOUT IT! NEXT CHAPTER. . . .

Columbo producer, Chris Seiter

the early days—
the fights—the
disputes—
the distrust

IT WAS VERY early in the history of *Columbo*. I'm talking maybe the first 35 days, and I earned a distinction that cannot be claimed by any other actor in the history of television. I was barred from the lot. I could not enter the gate of Universal Studios, and we hadn't even started shooting yet. This edict was issued by a studio executive to my lawyer, Bert Fields. I was stunned. Unbelievable. I'm playing the lead character. I'm the star, and I can't come on the lot.

Apparently the studio was responding to the producers, Dick and Bill, who felt (and I'm guessing at the words) that I was "interfering with their work"—getting the scripts out. But at that time, there were no scripts—not yet. There wasn't a specific scene or dialogue or anything that I had seen. Maybe they picked up on my known insistence on quality writing—my contempt for much of what is seen on TV—my refusal to deal with mindless action, dumb jokes, and exposition posing as real talk. At any rate, whatever Bert said, the ban was lifted in very short order.

in summit meetings called to settle disputes, where the star of a tv series sits can be decisive

IN THE EARLY days of *Columbo*, there was a big rift between me and the network and Universal Studios. It wasn't about money. That was already settled. I wanted to direct a *Columbo* episode. They said no.

My attorney, Bert Fields, set up a meeting in his office with myself, the head of the network who was flying out from New York, and the head of Universal Television.

Both men were prompt. Bert rose from his desk, greeting them. He gestured for them to take a seat, then nodded in my direction. I was lying on my back on the couch with a cold compress on my forehead. Bert told them I wasn't feeling well.

The cold compress was a wet washcloth. I got it from Bert's bathroom. It was a touch that occurred to me just moments before the moguls arrived. Bert and I both agreed that it completed the picture of someone not only sick, but feeling miserable—probably not in a good mood.

Bert opened the meeting by asking the network guy—we'll call him Marvin—how his flight from New York was. Marvin answered it was fine, and Bert complimented him on the network's most recent pilot. Marvin thanked him, said he was proud of his "crackerjack staff." During this exchange, I didn't speak or move—my eyes remained closed. Then one of the two moguls must have quietly, delicately inquired about me, because I heard Bert say, "He'll be fine."

At that point, without opening my eyes but sounding irritated, I said, "Can we get this show on the road?"

I couldn't see their reaction. I never once opened my eyes, but I was certain they were startled. They assumed I wasn't feeling well, but they never expected this level of irritation. They agreed quickly that the meeting should start. The two men instantly adopted a sympathetic manner. Using voices that were calm and reassuring, they pointed out that in any dispute, both sides have reasonable points. They went on somewhat more concretely to note the mutual benefits that result from on the one hand, A seeing B's position and on the other hand, B seeing A's position.

Somewhere around this point I interrupted: "Cut the bullshit. What is it, yes or no? Just say it."

This time Marvin responded vigorously and with some emotion, "Peter, you know as well as anybody that I have consistently and lavishly supported the *Columbo* show and I will continue—"

At this point, I'm off the couch and heading for the door, my head down, still holding the cold compress. Without looking up, just mumbling to the floor, sounding weak and miserable, I said, "I'm going home. Call me. Is it a yes or no? That's all I'm asking." And I was out the door.

Forty minutes later when I walked into my house, the phone was ringing. It was Bert. "Good acting. You should be *that good* on film. The answer is yes. You're directing the next *Columbo*. Don't throw away the washcloth."

peter falk's
ad-lib

IN AN EARLY episode with Bob Culp, Columbo gets his shoes wet in the opening investigation scene. He's interested in the chlorine content in the swimming pool in which the body was found. In order to put his finger in the pool so he can taste the water he steps onto the stairs leading into the pool and gets his shoes wet.

When Columbo first arrives on the scene, the detective already there has surmised the death looked like a diving accident; the body in the pool has an ugly wound on his skull and there's blood on the diving board. There are no witnesses, even though there was a big party the night before. These facts support the prevailing theory that after the party the victim, having had too much to drink, miscalculated his dive, hit his head on the board, and drowned.

The deck surrounding the pool has one area that's damp. This area is adjacent to where the body lay in the pool. The question for Columbo is whether that dampness is the result of the splash made by the body hitting the water, or perhaps made by water from a gardener's hose.

That's why he's interested in the chlorine content, why he tastes the pool water and why he got his shoes wet.

The next scene takes place later that day in the living room of the victim's house. The victim has recently inherited a top professional football team. All the principals—the victim's girlfriend, along with Bob Culp's character, who the victim hired to run the team (and incidentally the man who murdered him), Bob Culp's powerhouse defense attorney, and assorted police officials are all present. During an important speech by Culp detailing his whereabouts at the estimated time of death, Columbo taps the defense attorney on the shoulder and very quietly, unobtrusively whispering, asks the attorney a question—

COLUMBO
Excuse me, sir, how much did you pay for those shoes?

That question was not in the script—it was an on-the-spot impulse of mine. The thought of asking it tickled me and out it came. It also tickled a lot of viewers, too. I'd be walking down the street and people would come up and ask me regarding not only my shoes but anything I might be wearing—my tie, my pants, anything—How much did you pay for them?

Fast-forward fifteen years, and I'm doing an hour interview show on cable TV called *Inside the Actor's Studio*. This is a very popular show featuring actors talking about their careers. Some of the people I've seen on this show are Shirley MacLaine, Sean Penn, Carol Burnett, Chris Walken, Tommy Lee Jones, Anthony Hopkins, and Alec Baldwin.

The host, James Lipton, asks questions and the guest actor answers. They're both seated on stage talking to an audience of young theatrical students—actors, writers, and directors. The questions are good, the students are interested, and every show ends exactly the same way. Every guest actor is asked the same nine questions. For example:

HOST

What is your favorite word? What is your least favorite word? What is your favorite swear word? What profession other than your own would you like to attempt?

In my case, some of my answers went like this:

HOST

What turns you on more than anything else?

ME

When my wife loves me.

HOST

What sound or noise do you love?

ME

I like it when an old lady chuckles.

HOST

What sound do you hate?

ME

The squeal of brakes followed by the crash of steel.

HOST

If heaven exists, what would like to hear God say when you arrive?

ME

What did you pay for those shoes?

shera stories

THERE IS SOMETHING I have to get off my chest . . . and if the Lieutenant were standing here I'd say it right to his face. I'd tell him I take a backseat to no one in appreciation of your brilliance. What you see, what you hear, what you smell, how you find the answers—all that. But when it comes to wife stories I'd have to be honest and tell him the truth—Lieutenant, your stories about your wife don't hold a candle to my stories about my wife. For example, Shera (that's her, that's my wife) she had a running part on a TV series called *Maggie Briggs*. She played Suzanne Pleshette's roommate. Ken McMillan was the third member of the cast. Ken was an outstanding character actor I knew from my early off-Broadway days. One day Ken got into a heated argument with the show's director. The dispute grew, and the rest of the cast got involved. The voices grew louder—leading to:

KEN

Stop giving me directions. I don't want to hear them.

DIRECTOR

I'm just trying to have an intelligent conversation.

SHERA

This can't be an intelligent conversation.

DIRECTOR

Why not?

SHERA

Because I'm in it.

And here's another good one. One of the most popular attractions for tourists visiting Hollywood is the movie star home tour. Tourists pile into vans that drive them up and down the streets of Beverly Hills. The hope is that if you pass a celebrity home often enough—and the vans that drive past my place come by every fifteen minutes—you'll spot an actual star. The way this works is the driver slows down when he approaches the home of a celebrity. They keep an eye peeled, and if they spot an actor—or even his or her spouse—the driver immediately starts smiling and waving until he's pulled up close enough to offer a greeting in a tone suggesting familiarity. Anything to promote an exchange that will buy enough time for the folks in the van to snap their pictures.

One day Shera was out in the front of the house inspecting the paw of one of our dogs. He had something sharp embedded in his paw and Shera was concerned that he was in pain. The driver spotted my wife, slowed down, and assuming his most friendly tone attempted to initiate a conversation.

"Hi—nice to see you—how's Peter?"

Shera never looked up. "He died this morning."

Conversation over, back to the dog's paw.

You know how you walk into a room in your house and objects that have been in that room for many years don't stick out and hit your eye each time you pass through? A couple of years back, I walk into a room and it suddenly struck me—wait a minute—where are the Emmys? I knew they were kept in that room—I couldn't tell you the last time I remember seeing them, but there was a mob of them on the corner shelf.

I yelled to Shera, "Where are the Emmys?"

"They're in Aunt Linny's bedroom," she replied.

I went upstairs into Aunt Linny's bedroom, but I didn't see them. I called out to Shera that I didn't see them. She yelled back, "They're on the chest which is against the wall that faces the bed." When I looked at the chest, it took a minute to realize that the round black base which was visible under some hats was the base of an Emmy. Now it was suddenly very clear what happened. Shera, bless her heart, I could strangle her, was using the Emmys for a hat rack.

Shera had gone to a meeting with the producers of a TV show in regard to possibly playing a part in their next episode. I picked her up after the meeting, but she didn't look too excited getting into the car. "How did it go?" I asked. Shera made a face and answered, "They showed me the script and my character's first line is 'Working nine-to-five sucks.' I don't think the audience wants a character to say that word. I don't like that word and I don't like saying it. I told them to shove it up their ass."

When the Emperor of Japan was invited by President Carter to dinner at the White House, he was asked who he would like at his table. He said Columbo. I was shooting at the time and I regretfully had to decline. I was disappointed and so was Shera, which made the second invitation even more meaningful.

Two years later the Prime Minister of Japan, Masayoshi Ohira, was invited to dinner at the White House and he was asked who he would like at his table, and he also said Columbo. Both Shera and I were looking forward to this experience. We arrived in Washington in the late afternoon, went to the hotel, and got scrubbed up. Shera as usual looked fantastic. Now we were in a limo approaching the White House. The gates opened and we were heading up the driveway and there, brilliantly lit up against the dark evening sky, stood the President's house in all its magnificent whiteness. Shera turned to me and said dryly, "And you had to be an actor."

Sometime before we met, Shera was going with a guy. He was obviously crazy about her, and Shera told me that one day he announced that he wanted to buy her a gift. He said just tell me what you want and we'll go get it. Shera said she wanted a watch. Fine, he said, pick it out and I'll go get it.

That's what she did. She picked one out. It was a Piaget. She showed him a picture of it in a brochure—a full-page colored photograph along with the price. It was not cheap. The guy looked at the brochure. You could tell he was thinking. He took a beat and said, "What about this— what about I buy you a car with a clock in it."

The Films of
John Cassavetes

john cassavetes

THE WORLD HAS been making movies for roughly 80 to 90 years, and during that time we have seen an incredible parade of brilliantly talented actors, directors, and writers. However, the number of *"originals"*—artists who broke new ground—artists that presented to the world something the world had *never seen before*—these animals are rare. John Cassavetes was one of them.

John was an original. Considered by many to be the father of today's independent film movement, he was something Hollywood had never experienced before.

John created a new kind of film acting. He introduced into movies a new level of acting spontaneity that resulted in scenes that resembled actual life, as opposed to movie life.

What I noted above is generally acknowledged. What is *not* as well known is the originality of John's content, as opposed to his style.

In 1955, John made his first picture, *Shadows*. John, in his early twenties and without two dimes to rub together, makes his first picture. What's it about?—a love story between a black girl and a white guy. In 1967, *12 years later*, Hollywood, slapping itself on the back for its boldness in taking on this explosive issue, makes *Guess Who's Coming to Dinner* with Sidney Poitier—after John already did it.

Now it's the late 1970s—the revolt against the middle class—the obsession with success—with money—and what film is John making? He's making *Husbands*, a tale of three middle-class men who ride the commuter train each morning from a middle-class neighborhood in Long Island to their jobs in New York City. This picture is about the values of the American middle-class family—the bedrock upon which so much of our society stands.

Perhaps the reader will have a deeper, more visceral understanding of why I describe Cassavetes as an original if I describe the day John approached me about doing a play he was writing. He said it's about a standup comic who the audience didn't find funny. He wanted me to play the comic and he wanted my wife, Shera, to play his girlfriend. I asked where he intended to do the play, and he mentioned an abandoned little theater in a rundown section of West Hollywood. He told me he intended to personally do some remodeling at the theater, but his main focus would be the stage.

The design of the stage was going to be tricky, because he was not only going to write and do the play he offered me, he was going to write and do two other plays—and, mind you, do all three at the same time. Can you imagine that? Play #1 could be seen on Monday, Play #2 on Tuesday, and Play #3 on Wednesday . . . then on Thursday back to Play #1 and so on. That was a new one for me—never heard *that one* before. He would cast and rehearse all three plays at the same time. They would open the same week and run for one month. Tickets would cost one dollar. Nobody would get paid. Actors, backstage people, carpenters, box office—nobody would get paid. All volunteers. Gena Rowlands and Jon Voight would be in one of the plays, Shera and me in one, and at this moment I can't recall the actors in the third play. It will come to me.

It was an amazing experience. Nobody getting paid but everybody excited to be there. We all wanted to see the plays—to see how they turned out.

How did they turn out? Good question. I can answer it quickly and simply. Of all the movies that John created, I had one overwhelming favorite. It was John's last movie, *Love Streams*. I laughed and cried a lot. I loved it. *Love Streams* had been the name and story of one of the three plays. So my favorite movie of his was born on the stage. Turns out that experiment of doing three plays at once wasn't so wacky after all. It produced one of his best films.

Another outstanding play John wrote and produced was about a homeless bag lady. Gena played the lead, and if you think this was a depressing slice of realism about an unfortunate woman sleeping on concrete sidewalks, think again. There were scenes that included the royal family of Spain. Scenes that took place in Spanish palaces that included this homeless bag woman mixing with royalty and their circle of aristocrats. It was very funny and, like all of John's works, it ultimately packed an emotional wallop.

I should add that at the intermission the audience, while they enjoyed a cool drink and a cigarette, were treated to a homeless man who John found in downtown L.A. He played the spoons—and played them beautifully, I might add. The memory of that happy homeless black guy turning out that incredible music—that unique sound on those damn spoons—the beat so infectious, his whole body moving with it. I'll remember that dude forever. I'll remember him long after I've for-gotten the play. Question: Who but John would have thought of a homeless guy playing the spoons?

first meeting with john

THE FIRST TIME I ever spoke to John was at a Knick/Laker game. It was half-time, we were in the hot dog line, and we talked basketball for about three minutes, got our dogs, and that was it.

The second time had to do with *Mikey and Nicky*. That was an Elaine May script that I was crazy about. I was going to be Mikey, and both Elaine and I thought that John would be a sensational Nicky.

I called John. We met for lunch at Paramount Studios. I told him that Elaine wrote and would direct the script with me playing Mikey. We both wanted him for Nicky. I started giving him a very brief capsule indication of the characters, who knew each other as kids. Now in their 40s—they're both small-time racket guys. They worked for a bookmaker who also rented pinball machines.

At this point, John interrupted me. "I'll do it," he said.

I sat there staring at him . . . obviously irritated. I told him point-blank that both Elaine and I were serious about this project. It meant a great deal to us.

John replied, in a reasonable tone, "I said I'd do it. What else do you want?"

"I want you to ask some intelligent questions," I said.

That's all John needed. He took off. And, oh, what a performance. He had a strong voice. Other tables could hear him. "You think I'm like you—worried?!—anxious! Is it going to be a hit?"—"Will the critics like it?! Is my part good? Is your part better?" Two minutes of this—then a pause—then his finish—"Elaine wrote it and you're going to be in it. That's all I need to know." Then he sat down.

It took me a minute to collect myself, but I realized I was wrong. He meant it. He signed up. He agreed to play Nicky. That's what I wanted.

Peter with Ben Gazzara and John Cassavetes

I was wrong but I was happy. We had a pleasant lunch, had some laughs, were waiting for the coffee when John said, "I'm going to make a picture. I'm going to be in it, and I want Ben Gazzara in it. It's about these men from Long Island. They commute each morning to Manhattan. They're married—they're husbands. There are three of them. I'd like you to be one of them. What do you think?"

I just sat there—sat there shaking my head and smiling—I might have even chuckled. I looked at John—by now I was grinning—this man is something—he set me up pretty good. "I'll be one of the husbands," I said, and I put out my right hand.

He said, "I'll be Nicky," and we shook.

husbands

AFTER OUR MEETING in the Paramount commissary—after I agreed to do *Husbands*—what happened next? Nothing. Silence. I hear no more about *Husbands*. A year goes by, maybe two, not a word. I'm in Siberia making a movie—*Castle Keep*—Burt Lancaster, Sidney Pollack—I get a telegram, an offer to make a movie called *Husbands*. It's signed John Cassavetes, with a phone number in Rome.

I call him—what the hell is this telegram? He confirms the offer. But where's the script?! What's my part? I know nothing. Come to Rome; I'll answer your questions.

In Rome, in a hotel room, he tells me the story of *Husbands*. Nothing is written; he just talks. He goes from grand generalizations to specific scenes. Some scenes are very funny. I laugh a lot. Other sections are—unclear. I can't fit them together. That night we're with a group of friends in a restaurant. John tells the *Husbands* story again. He leaves out some of the best scenes—the ones I laughed at. He adds new scenes—some good, some not so good. From the hotel to the restaurant, it became a whole different script. Maybe in its essence it was the same movie. I couldn't tell. What *was* clear was John's incredible fertility.

Ben Gazzara was in Czechoslovakia making a movie. There was a political crisis and it became unsafe for Americans. His movie shut down. We three met in Rome. Our meetings were always the same: John talking, making up scenes. John insisting we join in. He wants the script to be a collaboration. He announced to everyone we three are writing the script together. Who remembers what I offered or what Benny offered. Bottom line, the story was John's—the structure was John's—the scenes were John's. Within those boundaries, Benny and I would improvise—some of which appears on the screen.

When the movie was over, I ask John what's this movie about? The critics and all the reviews saw three men who for the first time face their mortality—and suddenly hopping off to London was a last-fling attempt to hold on to their youth. Stuff like that.

John said, "Think of it this way: When you're an old guy, you can tell your grandkids about the time you and your buddies on impulse hopped a plane to London, spent three days drinking, gambling, picking up women, then came home to wife and kids." That's the way he described it. But the truth is that the two guys with good marriages come home; the third doesn't come home. He's in limbo. So for me, *Husbands* the movie is about the importance of family. I believe that was John's intention, but I wouldn't swear to it.

I did suggest that at the end of the movie, when John and I finally arrive home and are getting out of the taxi, we have two big bags of gifts and we have to sort out which ones are for his family and which ones are for mine—the singing duck with the umbrella is mine, the clown is yours. That was my grand contribution.

A NEW CHARGE
Justice Fortas and the $20,000 Check

'Husbands' on the Run
Peter Falk, Ben Gazzara
and John Cassavetes
make a movie

MAY 9 · 1969
40¢

the asian girl

One of my character's most memorable moments in the film is the hotel-room scene with the young Asian girl I pick up in a bar. The girl who played that part was in life very much like her character: lovely, shy, inexperienced. I'm not sure how much acting she had done, and *Husbands* might well have been her first movie. Her English was poor, and she was nervous about performing in a second language. Who wouldn't be? What could be tougher? Neither John nor I were pleased with the first footage we shot. The kissing scene in particular was disappointing.

What happened next could only happen on a Cassavetes movie. We went back to the hotel room one night after the day's work was done—just the three of us—John, the girl, and me. No crew—no one else. No equipment—just John's handheld camera. No blocking, either. John told the girl to move wherever and whenever she chose. He told me to do the same.

This was very liberating for both the girl and myself. It made a world of difference. The scene became alive. We followed our impulses. The girl was terrific and, by golly, wherever we went John and his camera was there catching all of the action. The footage we shot that night saved the day. It's in the movie, and it's outstanding.

a woman under the influence

TALKING ABOUT OUTSTANDING—I'll always remember a seven-minute stretch of acting on the movie *A Woman Under the Influence*. I was in the scene but I had nothing to do. Maybe one or two quick lines. Maybe at the end of the scene I pulled Gena Rowlands into my arms hoping against hope that physical contact would change things for the better between our characters.

The scene itself starts with Gena in the living room talking to me (her husband), her mother (played by John's mother), and her father (played by John's father). Gena started off sounding fairly normal. Obviously she was under some strain. Concerned about some incident involving the children.

A Woman Under the Influence (and we're not talking about booze) is a woman trying to please. Under the influence of her father, her husband, even her children. A woman who, to say the least, could use more self-confidence. That was Gena at the top of the scene, at the beginning.

Then in a beautifully crafted design she started shedding layers of normalcy. I watched transfixed. Right in front of my eyes I saw Gena descend into madness. Not suddenly but step-by-step. She shed one layer of normalcy at a time. With each new thought she appeared slightly wackier than in the previous thought. It was beautifully orchestrated. Totally unpredictable. Mesmerizing. Among the most memorable seven minutes of acting I have ever seen.

It's funny what you remember. Besides the scene I just described, what pops into my mind concerning *A Woman Under the Influence* is the first shot of the movie. It was a nothing scene. Nothing in terms of its difficulty. I was driving a truck into my driveway. The back of the truck was filled with seven guys—my construction crew. No dialogue—no nothing—just start the truck, turn right, and pull into the driveway. Somebody yells, "We're ready—Camera—Lights," and then John runs past the camera heading for the truck. The door window on the driver's side is open. John shoots his arm through the opening and jams a construction worker's hat on my head, turns, yells, "Action," and is gone.

I start the truck and we're moving but I'm mainly trying to see myself in the driver's mirror—to see how I look in my new hat. Turns out I didn't fully appreciate the "look" until after the shot, when I had time to study myself. What a kick! I loved what I saw. Believe me I looked great. That hat worked, really worked. It made the character. I was not only a construction worker—I was also the boss.

what is a cassavetes set like?

PEOPLE WANT TO know what's it like making a Cassavetes film. How is it different? Number 1: The work place on John's movies is looser. The set—that is, the stage—the place where you're filming is less formal. It's less structured.

On a big Hollywood movie, there is a very sharp demarcation between preparation—getting everything ready—and the actual shooting. Just before you shoot, there are four assistant directors plus their assistants, all yelling, "Quiet on the set." This yelling continues until you can hear a pin drop. Dead silence. Then and only then, the director's magisterial voice: "Lights, camera, ACTION!"

On John's pictures, a lot of times the camera would be rolling and I wouldn't even know it. I might hear John say, "Don't want to rush you, Peter, but we've been rolling for a while." That would make me laugh. I would say it's too noisy. He would answer, "Just start, I'll shut them up."

Incidentally, this is something I might have learned on John's movies . . . I act a lot better if I've had a good laugh just prior to the director's yelling "Action." And it makes no difference if it's a light amusing scene or a dark tragic scene. The important thing is that I'm free and loose and *available*. What's "available" mean? I'm totally open to be affected by only *one thing*—by what the other actor is doing or saying. I have no preconceived ideas—none. If I'm laughing, I'm not remembering any previous insights. Thank goodness. I'm not busy preparing a certain face or positioning my voice. I'm wide open, to the exclusion of everything else, to simply hear and see the other actor.

Don't get me wrong. This is not the way I felt when we first started the film.

Working on a Cassavetes movie was a totally new experience. No one made movies the way John did. For me and probably for Benny, this was all new, all different. I didn't always understand where we were headed, and I frequently wasn't sure where we had been, but it was always exciting, always alive. It could be infuriating, but never ordinary. In the end, it produced variety and spontaneity and made for a helluva movie.

getting
a laugh

JOHN AND I were at a Laker game, and John got into a beef with a guy seven rows in front of us. They were going at it pretty good, trading remarks—the crowd was now following their exchange when the guy in front suddenly turned, pointed at John, and said, "Do me a favor—go f__k yourself." John instantly shot back, "Stand up and say that." The guy stood up, 6'2", looked down at John, and said "Go F_ _K yourself."

John, ever the director, said, "Now sit down and say it."

The crowd roared—so did I—even the 6'2" guy broke into a smile as he started his downward journey.

John died in 1989. Roughly six months prior, sometime in 1988, a journalist (I've forgotten his name; we'll call him Bob) interviewed

John. He had no idea that John was ill, and it was only some time after they actually met and were talking that it occurred to Bob that John's days were numbered. Bob thought how terrific it would be if he could get this man at this stage of his journey to look back and reflect on his life—what he remembered—what he had learned—what was important—where are we all headed. The problem was, he didn't know how to broach the subject. How do you bring it up? What do you say? It was tricky. But he had an idea. He would ask a question about John's last movie (*Big Trouble*, starring Alan Arkin and yours truly, a sequel to Andy Bergman's inspired comedy *The In-Laws*), and he would phrase the question in such a way that it would serve as a platform for a second carefully phrased question, and by the third such question hopefully he would have eased John into talking about his life without ever asking him to.

BOB
John, your last movie—*Big Trouble*—what was *that* like? You write all your pictures—you have for 35 years—but this wasn't yours—you're directing something written by someone else— not only that, you're hired after the movie has been shooting for three weeks. My goodness—what was that like?

JOHN
Well, for starters I didn't have to worry about picking locations. That was all done—I liked that part—and, uh—

John took a pause—a rather long one—as he thought about his answer. Finally:

JOHN
It was difficult, but it was fun.

BOB
(*just wanting to be sure*)
You're talking about *Big Trouble?*

JOHN
No, I'm talking about my life.

———

I'm lucky because when it's time for me to meet my maker, John will have already set the standard—just follow his example—no one did it better.

I should point out that both John and I were in high school in the '40s, and most of the big male movie stars of that era—e.g., Clark Gable, Spencer Tracy, Tyrone Power, Eddie Robinson—had met their maker and were in heaven.

At any rate, it's now the late '80s, and I knew John was sick but I didn't know how sick. I should say I never squarely faced the question. To me, nothing really bad could ever happen to him—he was indestructible. Maybe John knew he wasn't, and maybe he felt it was time to set the record straight.

So we're on the phone, and John says, "I hear you're doing [blah, blah]"—he mentions some job—"Congratulations." I'm amazed that he knows this, because it was only that morning that I found out myself.

PETER
How do you know this! What are you, a witch?
I just found out myself this morning.

JOHN
Tyrone Power told me.

———

The reader knows that I've noted more than once that I'm sometimes in a daze—not that aware of what's happening around me—part of me is on the moon. Plus health-wise I've been lucky—I'm never sick, so I don't squarely face the reality that bad things can happen and maybe— just maybe—that's why John chose to tell me this story about his dog, Cosmo—his German shepherd.

Once again we're on the phone, and this is a few months after the Tyrone Power story, and John's condition—particularly in navigating steep hills and steps—is worse now than it was before. He's moving very slowly. Unfortunately, John's house sits above a very steep driveway, which weaves downward to the street and mailbox below. And for 11 years, whenever he went down to get the morning paper, Cosmo was with him, leading the way down and back up that steep hill. This dog and what he did is the reason John called me.

He began by telling me how considerate Cosmo was. He told me that when they went to get the paper that morning, Cosmo decided not to walk in front of him. It was embarrassing for John to be so slow and Cosmo knew this. Out of consideration for John's feelings, instead of being in front and a constant reminder to John of how slowly he was moving, Cosmo hung back out of sight, walking behind John's heels, and John appreciated that and noted it again.

JOHN

He showed me a lot of consideration. He's an unusual dog.
And when we got to the top of the driveway, you know what
he did? He went all the way back to the very end of our prop-
erty and when he finally got there, he threw up and died.
Peter, do you think he was trying to tell me something?

cassavetes—
a tribute

JOHN WAS VERY shrewd about money. He knew it was worthless. It only had one purpose—to help find a piece of film or a stage and try to capture life as he saw it.

John had a vision. He wasn't afraid, in the name of his obsession, to make a fool of himself. And if, as someone said, "Man is God in ruins," John saw the ruins, and he saw them with a clarity that the rest of us would find unbearable. But he was drawn to the God part, man's need for love, and he was always looking for a story that expressed the stupidities, weaknesses, foibles—that got in the way of that need.

Extraordinary people look at something and see three things, and the average person sees only one. John could see ten, and he was able somehow to put them all together. He housed in himself, under one roof, all the contradictions. He was a man of action, but also a dreamer. He was teeming with feeling, emotional, yet extremely intelligent. There are revolutionaries who want to tear down and make something fresh. Then there are the old-fashioned, those who see the wisdom in the past. John saw both. He was both. A complex man—he had antennae like Proust, but he was a competitor like Vince Lombardi. He was a wild animal, but at the same time the family was central to his universe. These are times when it's easy to be pessimistic. But if the tribe can produce somebody like John, there is still hope.

Gena Rowlands, John Cassavetes, and Peter

courtesy of Photofest

peter falk

Peter's wife Shera, the original party girl.

Peter's mother.

From left, Larry Rivkin, Louis Fishman, Mark Steinman, Barry Smooke, Ron Herman, Barry Sacks, myself, Andy Friendly, and Steve Chase. These are my golf buddies. They felt that a photo of them would be of interest to the reader. I didn't have the heart to tell them the truth. A quick glance—what's the harm?

Peter's birthday party 2005: top, David Leff, Melissa Leff, Lou Fishman, Ellen Fishman, Pam Dardik; bottom, Shera and Peter, and Arold Dardik.

My old golf buddy, Lee Wolfberg—terrific friend, lots of laughs. I'll miss Lee.

My friend Maureen Gaynor, whom I met when she was 7 years old—a member of the U.S. Disabled Olympics Seal team and my friend.

Christmas card 2002 with all the dogs.

Party photo directed by Shera. Standing, Lou Pitt; from left, Maurice Singer, Arold Dardik, Peter, and David Leff.

Carole Smith—officially my assistant—
however I can't imagine my life without her
—I love her. 1965–1980.

April Raynell—hit the jackpot again—
fabulous assistant—cream of the crop—
one of a kind—I love her. 1981–1995.

Janét Saunders—the Lord is good—all's
right with the world—the ship is steady.
How good is Janét! Fugeddaboutit—
she's the best. I love her.

Photograph by Stuart Bayer/*The Journal News*

Peter embracing schoolmate Bobby Yerks at the ceremony in which Prospect Avenue, Ossining, was renamed Peter Falk Place.

neil simon

I **FIRST MET** Neil "Doc" Simon sometime around 1960. He called me to set up a meeting. At the time, he wasn't the famous playwright whose brilliant comedies are celebrated all over the world. That would come in short order, with blockbuster hits like *The Odd Couple* and *Barefoot in the Park*. He was, however, at that time a top TV writer for stars like Sid Caesar and Phil "Sergeant Bilko" Silvers.

Who knows where Doc had seen me or why he would want to meet me? I was a totally obscure off-Broadway actor making a few dollars a week doing foreign playwrights in tiny back-alley theaters. To this day, I don't know how he knew I even existed. He must have seen me somewhere, because I have a definite memory of meeting him in his apartment. I have no idea what we talked about. Did I know who he was? I think so. I hope so. But I'm not sure. I was with him maybe 30 minutes, and then we said good-bye.

Fade out—Fade in. It's ten years later, and he offers me the lead in his hilarious Broadway play *The Prisoner of Second Avenue*. A terrific part in a terrific guaranteed smash hit play.

A couple of things stand out: The first day of rehearsal. I'll never forget that. We actors are on the stage, seated around a table with our scripts. Doc Simon and the director, Mike Nichols, are seated in the orchestra. The actors read the play straight through, page one to the end. The author and the director, Doc and Mike, clap politely, thank us, and head up the aisle for a pow-wow. Twenty minutes later, they return. The actors, now with coffee and doughnuts, are still on the stage. Coming down the aisle, Mike says they have an announcement. The third act is out—Wow! The cast is speechless, our mouths open.

Was the third act weak? Not by a long shot. Was the new one better? By a mile.

Doc wrote it in two days. Need I say more? Was this the big leagues, or what? Doc Simon and Mike Nichols—it can't get any better.

The play opened in Boston. It was sold out. Every seat and every performance thereafter in every city, it sold out. We were all terrific—Mike Nichols, Lee Grant, myself, the whole cast, but we were all replaceable except for Doc Simon. Without him, there was no baby. Without Doc, there was nothing.

The other thing I remember was how confident I felt coming back to the theater. I hadn't done a play in ten years; but being alone in that empty theater, walking around that stage, emerging from the seclusion of the wings into the full view of the live orchestra, felt good. I got a little tingle.

What I didn't anticipate and I should have? I'm so stupid sometimes. In the theater, you don't have a mike over your head. This is not the movies, Peter!!! You can't talk softly—you can't be conversational.

Nobody will hear you. There's no camera, no mike. Remember the folks in the balcony. They have to hear, too.

Mike Nichols, our director, was concerned about the sound level. One day, Mike said we'll run the first act from beginning to end, and he'll sit in the last row, and if at any time he can't hear, he'll let me know.

Mike goes to the back of the theater. The stage is empty. There is a beat of total silence, and I enter from the wings and say my first line. Mike says, "Can't hear you." I do some more business and say my next two lines, but I increase the volume. Mike says, "Louder." Lee Grant enters and says three lines. Mike says nothing, and then I increase my volume and say my fourth, fifth, and sixth lines. Mike says, "Can't hear you." I feel the anger rush through my body, and I deliberately just holler the entire next speech. I hear Mike say, "That volume is good—keep it right there." That's what he wants?! Okay. I just started shouting. I shouted the rest of the act and when it was over, I walked out.

That night, I had trouble sleeping. The next day, I had a beef with the cabdriver and words with the costume designer and then at the theater was curt to Mike Nichols when he arrived. Mike then came into my dressing room and asked me to sit down, which I did. He then said something I didn't understand. He said, "You're having an anxiety attack." I had never heard of that. I said, "What?" He repeated it. I told him I didn't know what he was talking about, and he handed me a pill. "What's that?" He said, "Valium." I said, "What?" He repeated it. I told him I'd never heard of it. What's it for? Well, he explained, and I eventually took the pill, and wow!—he was right. I got mellow, had a nap, and woke up relaxed and feeling on top of the world. But that's not the point.

I was 43 years old, had been to four colleges, made a film in Russia, would be recognized by Eskimos, was arrested in Havana, and knew Bette Davis. I didn't just fall off the Christmas tree, but I had never heard of Valium—never heard of an anxiety attack. There is a part of me that's on the moon. That's a simple fact.

A word about Lee Grant. In those days, I'm not sure what my life would have been like without Lee. She was the first guest star on a *Columbo*. Lee is an attractive, unusually desirable female. It's amazing at the drop of a hat how deadly she can become as a murderer—one of Columbo's most formidable adversaries. In *Prisoner of Second Avenue*, we were on stage together the entire play. She can be very funny. The audience loved her. She's a joy on stage and off. I love Lee Grant.

As it turned out, *Prisoner of Second Avenue* was a delight and a big success. From that point forward, I was Doc's for the asking.

—

As it turned out, we didn't work together for five more years. His next brilliant script came along in 1976. It was for the film *Murder by Death*, which was a knockout parody of those famous detective movies like *The Maltese Falcon* and the "Thin Man" series. The outrageous plot of *Murder by Death* concerns an eccentric millionaire—played wonderfully by Truman Capote, of all people—who invites the world's five greatest detectives to his secluded castle for "dinner and murder." The detective who solves the murder wins $1,000,000.

Added to this delicious premise was an all-star cast, the likes of which I'd not seen, not even in *It's a Mad, Mad, Mad, Mad World*. There was Peter Sellers in the role of Inspector Sidney Wang (*aka* Charlie Chan) who's given to terse observations ("conversation like television set on honeymoon: unnecessary"). David Niven and Maggie Smith played Dick and Nora Charleston (actually Nick and Nora Charles from *The Thin Man*). They're appropriately cool and above-it-all, even when faced by deadly scorpions crawling in their bed. James Coco was Milo Perrier, a spoof on Agatha Christie's Belgian private eye, Hercule Poirot—or, as

Peter in *Murder by Death*

Perrier says, "I'm not a Frenchie, I'm a Belgie"—with James Cromwell as Perrier's faithful chauffeur. Perrier's bit is that he's constantly eating. He doesn't care if he solves the case, so long as dinner is served on time ("Be quiet, everyone! I smell something."). There was also the incomparable Elsa Lanchester as Miss Marple and Estelle Winwood as her sidekick.

Naturally, a millionaire living in a remote castle would require a staff. He has a butler (Alec Guinness) who is prepared for a busy evening. His job is to escort each of the ten guests to their seats. Although he is blind, he's very familiar with the route from the front door to the dining room. Rounding out this extraordinary cast is Nancy Walker in the part of the maid, housekeeper, and cook. She is deaf and can't speak, but that doesn't interfere with her cooking. There were no complaints about the food. Last but not least, I played Sam Diamond (*aka* Sam Spade). Diamond came up the hard way, but don't be fooled. More than just a tough guy, he also has a fine, analytical mind. ("Locked from the inside. That can only mean one thing. And I don't know what it is.")

With such a stellar cast, you can imagine what a thrill it was for me to show up every day on the set. Peter Sellers was quite simply a genius. He could become anybody from any country at any age and probably any gender. And he did it effortlessly. No sweat, no push, just simply hilarious. The great Alec Guinness could be hilarious, too. He might rattle off a funny line then glide into a dramatic moment of towering agony from a Shakespeare tragedy. This went on all through production, and I loved every minute of it.

I find it amusing, though, that what sticks most in my mind after all these years are not the big moments but the small details. Like my chats with Truman Capote, for example. I once asked what he was writing at the moment. He said he had just finished a book. He had gone to different prisons and interviewed men on death row. I personally would have found that job interesting. Curious, I asked whether these condemned men had any one thing in common.

"There is one—but just one."

"What is it?"

"Tattoos."

Sounds right, doesn't it!

In spite of *Murder by Death* being a comedy, there was sometimes friction on the set. Every scene in a movie has to be lit. The Director of Photography (DP), his best boy, and his crew are the only individuals permitted on the set until the scene has been properly lit. Meanwhile, the actors are doing whatever, usually in their trailers reading, napping, or outside just talking. What frequently happens is that the Assistant Director (AD) will send for the actors before the set is completely lit. The actors then have to wait. Actors don't appreciate being called only to be kept waiting.

Peter Sellers was a bit touchy on this subject. I believe it was early in the shoot, maybe the first week, when Sellers was kept waiting for the first time. He told the AD he didn't like that and don't let it happen again. So the next week or so, Peter was called to the set at 8 o'clock. When he arrived, the lighting crew was still working. I happened to see Peter come onto the set. I was talking to Elsa, and I didn't notice where he went. Apparently 10 minutes later the AD was called to the phone and a guard at the main gate said that a man with a British accent asked him to call Stage 8 and leave a message: "Peter Sellers will be at home. Don't bother to call until after dinner." It goes without saying that was the last time Mr. Sellers was ever called to the set before they were actually ready to use him.

Murder by Death was a big hit, so Doc set to work on writing another detective parody of Sam Spade with yours truly back in the part of Lou Peckinpaugh. *The Cheap Detective* featured an outstanding line up of hilarious comedians in supporting roles, and the movie became a hit as well. That's what working with Doc was like for me: one hit after the next. I've played a lot of comedic parts over the years, some truly funny characters, but seldom ever have I laughed more than when making a Neil Simon picture. There's no one quite like Doc.

Peter in *Castle Keep* as Sfc. Rossie Baker

actors as artists

I **HADN'T REALIZED** until a couple of years ago, but James Cagney, Katharine Hepburn, Henry Fonda, Edward G. Robinson, Lionel Barrymore, Claire Trevor, Kim Novak, Jack Palance, Phyllis Diller—all drew or painted. There's even a book, *Actors as Artists*, that includes drawings and paintings from about seventy-five actors.

I was asked to be included in that book, and in that connection I had to answer some questions that made me think for the first time about how, when, and why I started drawing.

Back when I was in high school, there were two of us who could draw. Danny Gaultiere and me. However, Danny could draw from his imagination. He drew puppies, butterflies, people, whatever. He just made them up—didn't need a model. Not me. I could only draw something I could see. In my mind, Danny was the real thing. I wasn't in his league—there was something illegitimate about my having to look—compared to him I wasn't quite kosher.

Fast-forward to 1967, and I haven't drawn anything, not one line, in 25 years. I'm now an actor, and guess what. I'm working in Serbia, Yugoslavia. However, this time my job is not moving rocks from one pile to another. I'm working on a film starring Burt Lancaster, directed by Sidney Pollack, called *Castle Keep*. It's a war film, the actors are all males, it's winter, it's cold, it's Serbia. What do you do at night? You play poker.

That for me got old fast, so one night I quit the poker game early and went to my room. Sitting there alone, nothing to do but look at an old leather valise, and before I know it I've picked up a pencil and I'm drawing it. I remember the valise was soft brown Italian leather, I've had it for years, and I always liked its shape and texture.

The movie company was housed in a huge old castle, and a first-rate sculptor had his studio in the basement. One night he dropped by my room. "Who did these?" he asked, referring to my drawings of the valise. I told him I did, and he said they were pretty good. I thanked him but mentioned that I had had the valise right in front of me and was able to look at it the whole time I was drawing. He didn't answer immediately. It took him a moment to make sure I wasn't mentally defective, and he still looked somewhat incredulous as he pointed out that artists have been drawing from life since the beginning of time.

He must have thought he was talking to an idiot. At any rate, he set me straight. Some artists look more, some look less, some work from the mind's eye, others make stuff up. There are no rules, whatever I did was legitimate, and the results were pretty good.

drawing
art students' league

IT WAS NOW 18 months later. We've shot *Columbo*'s first season. We're on hiatus, and I'm living in Manhattan doing a Broadway play—*The Prisoner of Second Avenue*. Unlike working in Los Angeles on films, where you work during the day, and at night you have your family and friends, working in New York theater means your job is at night, and during the day you have your hotel room but your family and friends are not in it. So what do you do all day?

My hotel was on 58th Street, and I must have walked down 57th Street a hundred times. A couple of blocks from my hotel was an old building—a sign read art student's league. One day I stopped and went in. It was very quiet inside, no one in sight. I pass a closed door. I stop, return to it, and quietly open it just enough to see in. Wow! There she is—up high on a platform, her weight on her right hip, her shoulders back, nipples thrust forward. Lit from above, the glow on her hair, buck naked, and absolutely still. A model being drawn by students. Right there on the spot, I knew what I was going to be doing starting early tomorrow morning: drawing women—hair up—hair down—clothes on—clothes off. The most fascinating subject known to man.

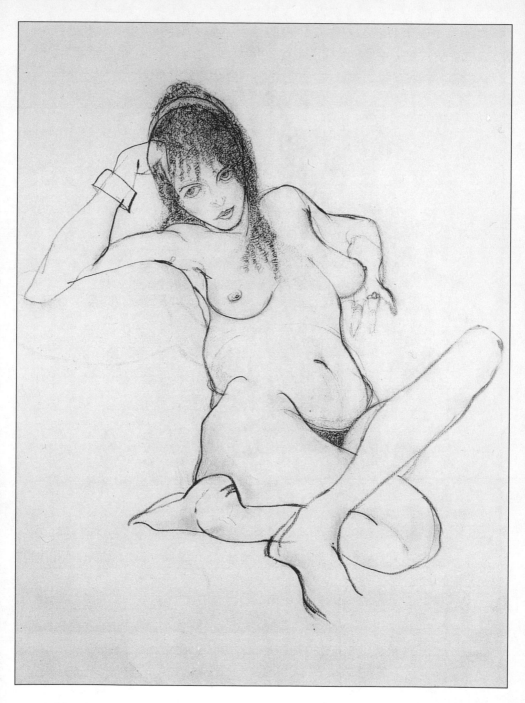

Margo

Claudia Lost in Thought

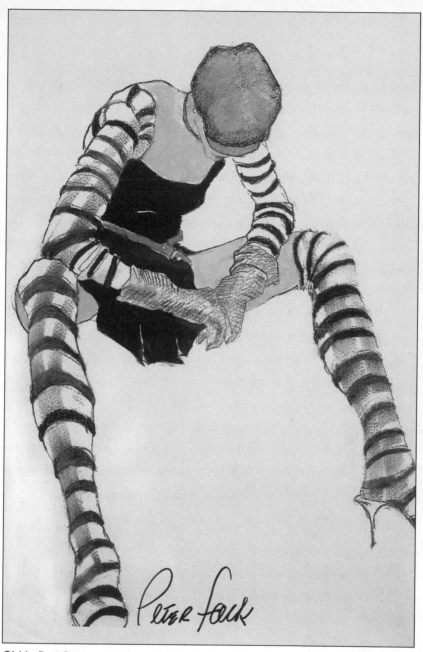

Girl in Red Cap

I got hooked on cigarettes when I was 15, and I tried some pot when I was 18 on a beach in Buenos Aires, but pot never got to me, so maybe smoking, golf, shooting pool, and acting were the only things that grabbed me the way drawing did. The theater was five blocks from the art school, so if I wasn't in my dressing room by 7:30 the stage manager knew where to find me in order to make the 8:00 curtain. I was so hooked on drawing, I would frequently schedule a session for after the show, starting around midnight. The TV writer and playwright Paddy Chayevsky loaned me his office above the Carnegie Deli on 55th Street. The model would come there, and that session would end around 2:30 a.m. If you're thinking I was a bit crazy, you're right. But not certifiable.

Unfortunately, the drawing binge ended when I had to return to Los Angeles to start the new season of *Columbo*. So much for having my days free. But whatever the interval—two months, five months, or four times a year—my appetite to draw stayed strong.

So why did I wait forty-four years to take up drawing? I believed my delay was related to that naïve notion that having to look while you're drawing was somehow cheating. However, claiming that naïveté is involved is a tough sell. It sounds too dumb. Instead I see a definite pattern of delays in my life:

1. It took twelve years for me to decide to become an actor.

2. I didn't get married until I was 32.

3. It took 43 years for me to take up drawing, and another 31 years to go to watercolor.

In case you, the reader, feel I'm exaggerating when I say "there's a part of me that's on the moon," hear this story. When I was thirteen years old, I attended my first wedding. Right after the ceremony, there was a terrific commotion and I saw people moving quickly toward the back yard. "What's going on?" I asked a pretty girl who ran past me. She turned around and shouted excitedly, "They're going to throw the bouquet." What's the fuss? I didn't understand. She yelled back, "Whoever's up front has the best chance of getting the bouquet first." Well, I ended up not in the very front but close enough to get a good start. I was quicker than the others and stronger—in fact I was surprised how easy it was for me to shove aside, or in some cases knock down anyone who was in my way. It was only after I caught the bouquet and saw every-one looking at me, some doubled over in laughter, that I realized all the bodies I had knocked down were women.

Autumn Promenade

a message
to the people
of romania

THE PHONE RANG. The voice said he was from the
State Department. He was calling from a suite in the
Beverly Wilshire Hotel. The American ambassador to
Romania was with him. He wanted to know if I could join him and
the ambassador in his suite. This sounded crazy, like a gag, but I
have to admit I was curious. For some reason, I didn't think it was
a gag—but what else could it be? "This meeting—what's it about?"
I asked.

He answered firmly, "It's not something I care to discuss on the
phone."

Very weird. But I was dying of curiosity. He sounded like he
could be from the State Department. Then it occurred to me—
maybe they have the wrong person—they think I'm somebody
else. I asked, "Do you know who I am?"

He said, "Yes."

"Who?"

"You're Peter Falk."

I'm thinking: what do I do now?

"We're in 1503–1504, fifth floor."

I heard myself say, "Okay, I'll be there soon."

Now I'm thinking . . . should I change my clothes? If I do, what do I change into? The State Department guy sounded pretty crisp. He could be in tails. On the other hand, this could be a kidnapping. Screw it. I'm going, and I'm wearing what I've got on.

I was on the fifth floor, outside Room 1503–1504. I rang the bell. The door opened, and a servant silently gestured for me to come in. From the foyer, I could see the right half of the living room. Was that a TV camera?? I moved forward quickly. "Turn that camera toward the wall, away from me."

The camera operator didn't move until someone with a commanding voice spoke a few foreign words and the camera was turned toward the wall.

A tall man with a trim, thin mustache strode up to me and introduced himself as the man from the State Department. He was followed by our Romanian ambassador, who offered his right hand, as did a third gentleman who didn't speak English. They reassured me that the camera was not operating and one of them, in what could have been an attempt to lighten the mood, asked, "You don't by any chance speak Romanian?"

I wasn't ready to smile. I just said, "No."

"Well, you could have fooled the Romanian people. They all think you speak Romanian."

"And the French think I speak French—and the Germans think German. What else is new? And what's on those cue cards?" I was referring to huge four-foot-by-four-foot white cardboard cue cards with black letters on them.

A crewmember was stacking them near the camera. "That's phonetic Romanian," the ambassador said. "Those are letters from the English alphabet. If you pronounce them in English, they will sound like a Romanian word. For instance . . ." and he pronounced in English the first five words. "That's Romanian for 'You know me, I'm Columbo.'"

"What else does it say?" I asked coldly.

The Romanian man, sounding very Romanian, pronounced the next few sentences. The ambassador translated them into English. Roughly remembered, the words said, "I'm here to tell you that you should trust your government. It tells you the truth. Believe me when I say that."

I took a beat—let the silence speak for a few seconds; and then, sounding genuinely thoughtful, I queried, "What, gentlemen, if I may ask, what in God's name, and please excuse the language, what the fuck do I know about the Romanian government?"

The ambassador, simply ignoring my last remark, replied pointedly, "Your last *Columbo* started shooting in L.A. on October 1, 1973 and finished 20 days later on October 28. Your previous *Columbo* started July 15 and finished August 13. I got that information from the Romanian government. The fact is that that government has precise information on every *Columbo* you've ever made." Now his main point.

"The fact is, the *Columbo* show has swept the Romanian nation. The entire population is addicted to it. Columbo is Romania's Elvis Presley. They love him—can't get enough of him—and that's the problem. That's why we're turning to you. Do you want to hear more?"

"I'm sorry. I didn't realize. Please continue."

"Romania has strict quotas limiting the amount of American TV allowed in the country. These quotas have nothing to do with *Columbo*, BUT you only make six *Columbos* per year. That's a small number—very small, BUT that's all the people get to see—six, just six. And the people think they know why. They think they only get to see six because of the quotas. The quotas are to blame. Lift the quotas, and they'll see 26. The government tells them—not once, but ten times—there are no quotas for *Columbo.* Nobody believes it. Who believes the government? Nobody! Who will they believe? You! They'll believe Columbo."

Finally I understood what this was all about. Naturally I said yes. I was flattered. I heard myself instructing 10 million Romanians—"Trust your government. Why? Because Columbo said so." I felt very important. Am I an international luminary, or what? You bet your ass I am. Top that, Seinfeld!

can movie directors
help movie actors?
if so, how?

WHEN ACTORS GET together over dinner or at a bar, they've been known to talk about directors. This director is annoying, he never shuts up. Or that one is neurotic, and the other one is funny, I liked him, he relaxed me. They'll have stories to illustrate their point.

I have a story I like to tell, and from the look on the other actors' faces, I can see they've never heard a director story like mine.

The movie was *Mikey and Nicky,* written and directed by Elaine May. (It's recognized that Elaine is uniquely gifted, and everyone includes her among just the handful of genuinely original voices in the business. She's also one hell of a director. Listen to this.)

Cassavetes played Nicky and I'm Mikey and we're both small-time racket guys—illegal entrepreneurs—we book bets—we fence stolen goods—we monopolize slot machines. We have a complicated emotional relationship. Mikey is emotionally inhibited and wishes he could loosen up. He knows he's too earnest. He wishes he could be like Nicky. People are drawn to Nick. He's fun to be with and women adore him. When Mikey goes out with him, Nicky attracts the women and Mikey has a good time. Mikey wishes that they were best friends. He worries, however, that if he were in trouble Nick wouldn't do for him what he knows he would do for Nick. His anxiety is justified because Nicky has a psychopathic streak. He seduces people, but then he can't help himself and screws them over. So Mikey alternates between looking forward to being with Nick and wanting to strangle him with his bare hands.

One night, after their friendship has been put through an extremely stressful period of suspicion, they find themselves reconciled and laughing like two kids.

Nick says he knows a girl who "puts out"—they should go see her and Mikey will have a great time. The girl lives in a tiny one-room apartment with a closet-sized kitchenette. Nick, on the couch with the girl, "goes first" and Mikey, uncomfortably sitting on a small stool in the 2 x 4 kitchen, can see and hear everything that is happening on the couch. He hears Nick in heat repeating "I love you," and the girl's groans.

When he's done, Nick heads for the kitchenette, gesturing for Mikey to take his turn. Mikey is uncomfortable. He doesn't want to go. He tells Nicky, "She's your girl. I heard you tell her you love her." Nicky waves that off. "Everybody tells her that—that's what she wants to hear—go ahead—just tell her you love her—it will be fine."

Mikey approaches the girl tentatively. He sits beside her on the couch. Their thighs touch. He feels he should start by complimenting her, so he says, "It's unusual for a girl to be both pretty and intelligent." He's referring back to an earlier comment of hers that she likes to listen to the news and that the Chinese have a big army.

John Cassavetes and Peter as Nicky and Mikey.

It's still awkward between them, but Mikey feels she liked what he said, so in a very nice way he asks her for a kiss. She demurs and he asks her again. Once more she declines. He puts his hand gently on her shoulder and moves his head forward, his lips touching hers. His eyes are closed, so he doesn't see anything, but he hears his scream as she bites down savagely, sinking her teeth into his lip.

He's humiliated, but even deeper is his rage—not at the girl, but at Nicky. He knows that Nicky has set him up. This girl is no whore. Nick knows that. He knew what would happen. The minute they hit the street outside her apartment, Mikey can't wait to confront Nick—to take him on. He has a laundry list of grievances going back to when they were kids, and this was going to be his moment.

The scene just described in the apartment where the girl bites Mikey's lips was shot, say, on Monday and its continuation, the scene that follows in the street outside her apartment, was shot maybe ten days later.

This is a climactic, beautifully written, but emotional, funny scene, and I felt the first take left a lot to be desired. However, considering that we had to pick up where we left off a week before and recapture a complex set of emotions, I wasn't surprised at a weak beginning. However, the next two or three takes were no better, and we were getting ready for another one. The Assistant Director had yelled, "Quiet," then called out, "Camera." We were waiting for "Action" when Elaine said, "Just a minute. I want a quick word with Peter."

I'm fond of Elaine. We've been friends for years. She's very smart, and I was looking forward to hearing what she had to say. She was very near now, but because there was crew around she half-whispered, "I want to remind you of something." I could tell she wanted to talk confidentially so I leaned into her. We were very close—our arms around each other's waist, our heads cheek-to-cheek, but before I heard her words I felt something—I'm not sure what. There was a split second of total confusion—I didn't know what was happening. Then I was almost certain that what I was feeling was Elaine's teeth on my lip. My first thought was this is a gag, but then it started to hurt and I was about to push her when she suddenly, savagely, sank her teeth as deep as they could go into my lip. I was in the middle of my scream when I heard Elaine in her small voice say to the cameraman, "Action."

Well, did that scene sing. What a take! I loved it. I was really good. And when Elaine yelled "Cut" and the shot was over, I still didn't fully comprehend what had just happened. I just remember feeling good—elated—and in awe of what Elaine had done. That's what I would call a "Hall of Fame" director. Thank you, Miss May, you are—it's true—uniquely resourceful.

Elaine May

on why i wasn't in *the godfather*

AL RUDDY WAS a producer on *The Godfather*. The project had HUGE written all over it from the moment it was announced. The film was based on Mario Puzo's bestselling novel, and Marlon Brando had already committed to the lead under Francis Ford Coppola's direction. The whole town was talking about *The Godfather*, so when Al Ruddy called, believe me, he had my attention.

Al was no stranger—he had been to the house (he had dated one of Alyce's friends) he had a good sense of humor. He told me Coppola and the producers wanted me in the movie; in fact, according to Al, the whole room got excited when my name came up in a casting meeting. My character's name was Moe Green, a Las Vegas mobster. After all these years and films under my belt, back to a mobster again. However, this wasn't just another movie.

Al sent me the script. I started reading and knew right off the bat that the picture was going to be sensational. I was also on the lookout for my character. However, when I finished the script, I hadn't run across Moe Green. Could I have missed it in all my enthusiasm? I read more closely the second time, and still no Moe Green. Finally, I spotted him on the third reading. He had a few lines in a casino scene toward the end.

I wanted so badly to be in the movie, but the part was just too small for me to play. I owed Al a call, but I decided I'd get something out of this, even if it was just a chuckle. So rather than call Al back, I did nothing, knowing that I would hear from him shortly. A week passed and sure enough, Al phoned:

"What happened? You were supposed to call," he asked.

"Let me explain, Al. This movie is going to be huge—it's going through the roof. I was excited to be sent the script—I couldn't wait to read it, you understand."

"Of course."

"I'm still excited; that hasn't changed."

"Good."

"There's just one problem," I said. "Nothing that can't be fixed."

"Okay. What's the problem?"

"Al, be patient. I'm on it—can you give me a day?"

"For what?"

"I got a private investigator coming in. . . ."

"An investigator?! For what?"

"I can't find the part."

why marlon brando
wears an earplug

FOR US ACTORS, there is only one "Man." Marlon he be "The Man." He's the best—the baddest, and whatever he says or does is of interest to the rest of us.

To give you a better idea of what I'm talking about, I'll give you just one example. Brando made a picture called *Mutiny on the Bounty* in 1962. Although I had never seen the movie until recently, I had heard a terrific story years ago about Brando's solution to a specific acting challenge. Apparently Brando had to play a scene in the movie where his character (Mr. Christian) was deathly ill from a fever that produced a high temperature and uncontrollable shivering. According to witnesses, Brando asked for a cake of ice that would be big enough for him to lie down on. And that's what he did. He laid on the block of ice in order to help produce shivering. When I heard the story, I was bowled over by Brando's ingenuity. Who'd have thought of that? Lying down on an actual block of ice? When the movie came on TV not long ago, I kept my eye peeled, as I didn't want to miss the scene. Well, I'm here to tell you—it was fan—tas—tic.

Now it's 1995, and Brando is acting in another picture, *Don Juan DeMarco*, with John Depp, Faye Dunaway, and my friend for 55 years from Syracuse University, Bobby Dishy. Bobby lives in New York; but when he works in L.A., there's a good chance he can be found at my house. At any rate, all of Bobby's scenes are with Brando, and he would tell me how loose Brando was, mischievous like a kid, and kept everybody laughing. Then his tone changed, and I could see he was really interested in what he was about to ask me.

BOBBY

Did you know that Brando never memorizes his lines?
They feed them to him—he hears them in his ear—
like a telephone.

FALK

I heard that—but I didn't know if it was true.

BOBBY

It's true.

FALK

How does it work?

BOBBY

When the scene starts someone, somewhere behind the
camera, speaks Brando's lines into a microphone and the
words are transmitted directly to his earpiece.

FALK

Why does he do that?—I heard actors say he does it because
he's too lazy to learn the lines.

BOBBY

I don't buy that.

FALK

Ask him.

courtesy of Photofest

A couple of days later Bobby showed up. He had asked Brando. This is the gist of what Brando told him.

For openers, the lines he's not memorizing are not written by William Shakespeare, nor for that matter Tennessee Williams—but that's a small point. The main reason Brando does it this way is that it makes him less conscious of the camera. *Boy, did that ring a bell.* I immediately knew exactly what Brando meant. Actors are like everyone else. Everyone loses spontaneity when a camera is pointed at them. We all tighten up—become self-conscious.

When that big bad camera is inches away from your nose and staring directly into your eyes, you'll do anything to minimize its presence—anything to take your mind off the camera and onto something that interests you. And what could interest an actor more than finding out what he's supposed to say—discovering on the spot his next thought—and however he's affected, his reaction will be fresh, sudden, spontaneous. Obviously, it's more involving to listen and on the spot discover what you're about to say and feel than to already know not only what you are going to say, but how you're going to say it. Anyway, before I beat this point to death, I feel the same way about the plug in the ear as I do about the cake of ice: I wish I had thought of it.

If you asked me how I prepare for a part, I'd tell you I belong to the Swoosie Kurtz school of acting. I once heard her asked in an interview how she prepares for a role. Swoosie said that regardless of the part, she always asks the same question; "How did I do it last time?" That sounds like me.

the brink's job

SHORTLY BEFORE 7:30 P.M. on the evening of January 17, 1950, a group of armed, masked men emerged from 165 Prince Street in Boston, dragging bags containing $1,218,211 in cash and $1,557,183 in checks, money orders, and other securities. These men had just committed the "Crime of the Century," the "Perfect Crime," the fabulous Brink's robbery.

Twenty-eight years later, in 1978, Dino De Laurentiis hired Billy Friedkin to direct—and myself, Peter Boyle, Warren Oates, and Gena Rowlands to act in—a movie based on the most sensational robbery in American history.

A word about our director . . . Billy Friedkin burst upon the Hollywood scene like an exploding comet. He came to L.A. and, in what seemed like minutes, turned the town upside down with his smash 1971 hit film *The French Connection*. A mere two years later, he followed up with another earthshaking, record-breaking smash hit, *The*

Exorcist. His third picture, based on a famous French thriller, *Wages of Fear*, was a dud—poor reviews and even poorer box office sales. This was a big disappointment for both the industry and Billy—naturally, the whole town was poised for another big hit.

Fade Out and Fade In—it's 1978, and it's Billy Friedkin's first day directing *The Brink's Job*. The first scene takes place at night. It's 7:15 p.m. movie time. There are five thieves in a car, two in the front and three in the back. The leader, Tony Pino, whom I played, gives each man his final instructions in hushed tones. It is now 7:18, and in two minutes Tony will drive three blocks and park. There the men will jump out of the car with their guns, and the robbery will begin.

If you, the reader, were inside that car with the five actors, you would feel their tension—that tightness in their stomachs, that typical opening-shot queasiness. All actors feel it on their first shot of any movie.

We heard the Assistant Director yell "Quiet," then "Places," then "Camera," but instead of the next command, "Action," we heard Billy Friedkin yell "Hold it—stop—I want to talk to the actors." He ran over to the car. I opened the driver's-door window, but he ignored me and opened the whole door.

"I got your motivation for this scene . . ." he said. We all leaned in eager to hear. "I need a hit!"

It only took a second, then the five of us in the car burst into laughter—tension gone.

I will now tell you what happened on this movie that had never happened before on any movie in the history of movies. This was a caper movie, and Billy apparently knew personally two guys who were professional thieves. They were the real article. They had been robbing for years—big jobs—little jobs—they both did time—jails and prisons. I'm not sure how Billy expected them to help—maybe demonstrate how to pick a lock—how to blow a safe—but they were on the payroll. I personally don't recall any professional contact with them, but socially we all knocked around together. Everything was fine until, one day, the two robbery consultants were gone. They were let go. None of us knew why, only that they were gone.

Three weeks later, the two fired ex-robbery consultants walked unexpectedly into the editing room with guns. This was no demonstration on how to hold up somebody. One look at the editor's face when he felt that gun muzzle pressed against the base of his head was all you needed to see. The terror in his face said it all—this was the real thing. The editing room was full of cans of film, which they stole. Every last can.

The cops arrived. Detectives everywhere. The cast and crew were in shock. The editor's family arrived. His wife broke into tears when she

Peter as Tony Pineo.

courtesy of Photofest

hugged her husband. There were rumors of a telephone call. Then we heard that the thieves were looking for ransom money. We were herded into the courtyard of our hotel. Dino De Laurentiis arrived. Speaking into a microphone, he told us he had heard from the crooks. They want a half million dollars in ransom money. They want the exchange of money and the return of the film to take place tomorrow. Then Dino, in broken English, said the following:

DINO

I no like pay so much money—I say them half million too much. I no pay. I say I pay money but no so much. I say I pay 10 dollar—then I say no—too much—I pay five dollar.

By this point Dino is laughing very hard.

He passes the mike to the police commissioner. The commissioner explains that what the thieves took was only developed film. *BUT* they didn't get the *NEGATIVE*—not one frame. The negative is *not* in the editing room. The negative is locked in a vault in the laboratory—not one frame missing. So what the thieves stole is worthless. It can be reproduced in a matter of hours.

The old adage "Truth is stranger than fiction" certainly applies here. Talk about the gang that couldn't shoot straight. Who would believe that professional thieves could be that dumb? Sounds like something *I* might do. Being that unaware, living on the moon, sounds like me, not an experienced lifelong professional thief.

However, wait a minute, hold the phone, I just remembered something—something I read in Noel Behn's book—I think it was there— wherever, makes no difference—this is rich—this is pertinent. . . .

The actual robbery of Brink's took place in January 1950. But according to a book by Noel Behn titled *The Big Stick-Up at Brink's*, one year prior to that, Tony Pino and his boys had done their research and designed their plan and had scheduled the robbery. When I say they had designed their plan, the reader cannot possibly appreciate the depth, the thoroughness of their plan. To appreciate that, one has to know Tony Pino. He considered himself one of the world's top thieves. He had a dream. He was obsessed. He wanted to be the architect of the greatest robbery in American history. He wasn't some assbucket wild man walking into a bank waving a gun. He was a mastermind genius with an obsession.

Only Tony hadn't completely done his homework. Let's say the robbery was to hit Brink's on a Wednesday at 6:00 p.m., not totally dark outside, but sharply reduced visibility. Let's say it's 5:30 and all the thieves had taken their stations—one was on the roof of the building across the street facing the main entrance to Brink's, one was standing in the street dressed like a window washer who had taken off his gear and was leaning against his truck, and let's say a third guy was on another roof with binoculars that could spot the arriving Brink's truck. From another roof, another spotter was waiting for the changing of the guards on the second floor. Another was waiting for the 5:50 p.m. Brink's patrol car to pull into the parking lot. So everything was set, everything was in place; but then strange things happened, or didn't happen. . . .

The patrol car never arrived, there was no changing of the guards, and the Brink's truck never showed up—nothing that was supposed to happen happened. Why? The reason is simple: *BRINK'S HAD MOVED!* Can you top that? Moved! They were now in another building, eight miles away. So that old saying, "The best-laid plans of mice and men . . ." sure suited this occasion.

I feel I should spend a little more space on Tony Pino. Tony was "a piece of work." Here's how he prepared the plan to rob Brink's in their new location. He found a vacant office on the third floor of a building opposite the Brink's building. Locks were no problem for him—he could break into anyplace. Every day and night for three consecutive months, he was in that vacant office casing Brink's. From his vantage point, he could see what was happening inside the building and obviously all movement of cars, trucks, and people outside the building. He had binoculars, his pencil, and notebook—and one other thing. Before he left his house each day, he would empty a milk bottle and put it into his briefcase along with pencils, erasers, and notebook. He did this because once he was seated at his station watching Brink's, he didn't want to miss anything, not even for a second. That's why the empty milk bottle was important. If he had to piss, he did it right into the bottle without leaving his chair.

Some of the other guys who actually pulled off the original robbery were also on the payroll of the movie; at least I think they were. They were certainly around a lot and they loved talking about Tony. Apparently Tony had figured a way to get into the new Brink's building. There was no one there after, say, midnight, and he loved going there and just hanging out, looking at everything, but the other guys after twenty visits had had enough. A guy named Jazz Mafia would say, "That goddamn Tony would call me at two o'clock in the morning, 'Jazz, let's go over there.'"

"I'm sleeping, you dumb bastard. We were just there last night."

"Come on," he'd say, "we'll use their phone, call long distance."

So these guys spent a lot of hours actually hanging around inside the Brink's building prior to the actual robbery. But even Tony could make a mistake. Once again, they set a date to hit Brink's. It was set for a Thursday night, and everything was fine through Wednesday, but something happened Thursday afternoon. They had to postpone. What happened? Tony got picked up for shoplifting. He was stealing golf balls. As I said, this guy is a piece of work.

the in-laws

THE FUNNIEST PICTURE I ever made was *The In-Laws*. If you asked four people, seven of them would include *The In-Laws* in that rarefied list of "all-time funny pictures." And of the seven, there would be ten that would say that the funniest scene in this very funny picture was the serpentine scene.

Today when I'm walking the streets in a crowded city, the chances are that within four blocks some taxi driver will slow down, open his window, yell "Serpentine," give me the thumbs-up sign, and wave good-bye chuckling—or four construction workers three stories up on an unfinished roof will spot me and all four in unison will shoot an arm straight upward toward the sky, shout "Serpentine," and laugh hilariously.

This scene obviously struck some universal chord in the human funny bone. At every screening, "Serpentine" always gets roars.

Knowing this, I think the reader will find it interesting to hear a short two-line conversation that Alan Arkin and I had just prior to the first time the scene was shot. We were waiting for some last-minute camera adjustments. I had a question that I had been waiting to ask, and this seemed a good time.

PETER
(*to Alan*)
Alan, I have a question.

ALAN
Yes.

PETER
Do you think this is a funny scene?

ALAN
(*not believing his ears, looking incredulous*)
And you don't?

PETER
No. I think it's silly.

ALAN
You're the dumbest actor in America.

Looking back, I'm amused at the memory of being so wrong. For some reason, I actually like myself for being so stupid. And get this—I really enjoyed—no, I loved, actually—performing the scene, and I'll tell you why. Alan loved that scene so much. He got such a kick out of just doing it. Watching him, his total enjoyment, his funny run five steps left, then five steps right, all the while yelling "Serpentine"—he could have done that run a hundred times—he'd still be doing it today if the crew hadn't gone home. It tickled him so much. And watching him tickled me.

Peter and Alan Arkin arriving at the wedding in *The In-Laws*

how
the in-laws
began

WHILE WE'RE ON *The In-Laws*, the reader might be interested in hearing how the project started. What's the first thing that happened— for me, that is—not for Andy Bergman, the author, whose mind's eye first saw these scenes, these people, these insane wildly funny events that he somehow miraculously turned into not just a coherent story—but an inspired totally brilliant comedy. I don't know how it began for Andy or for that matter Alan Arkin, but for me it began with a call from the agent saying that Columbia Pictures wants to do a remake of *Freebie and the Bean*.

What's *Freebie and the Bean*? Good question. That was a movie starring Alan Arkin and Jimmy Caan playing cops. That's how *The In-Laws* began. They want to remake a story of two cops. Nothing could be further from *The In-Laws* than a cop story. Hard to believe, but that's what they wanted. With this in mind, I was asked to meet with Alan

Arkin. "Absolutely," I replied. I never mentioned that I never saw *Freebie and the Bean*. Everybody assumed I did, so let sleeping dogs lie.

We met in Alan's hotel room. It wasn't a long meeting. I was there for only a few minutes when he asked me straight out: "Peter, do you want to do a remake of *Freebie and the Bean?*"

I was surprised by this question. I thought that was why we were meeting. I left out that I had never seen *Freebie and the Bean* but honestly said, "If that's what they want, it's okay with me. I would certainly look forward to working with you, Alan."

Two things became clear immediately from Alan's response. He was not wildly excited about a remake of *Freebie and the Bean*, but he did believe we would make a good team, which was something he would look forward to. He added something specific which struck me because it was something that never occurred to me. He said if we make a "buddy" picture, it should be about two guys who don't know each other, who have no past together, who have just met for the first time. In theory, that sounded fine to me, and that was our first meeting.

I'm going to guess since I don't remember exactly but let's say four months later, the telephone rings and it's Alan from New York.

ALAN
Peter, I got the script. It's terrific and you have the best part.
The movie title is *The In-Laws*.

For anyone who's seen the film, you can imagine my delight, laughing myself silly as I turned the pages, and roaring with laughter and pleasure at the ending.

For those of you who haven't seen *The In-Laws*, I should point out that in the movie the two lead characters don't know each other and early in the story meet for the first time. Why in our first meeting—four months before I received the script—why did Alan say it would be better if our two characters didn't know each other?—They should meet for the first time. To this day I've never asked Alan why he said that. Why should I ask? He had his reasons. Let sleeping dogs lie.

courtesy of Photofest

the in-laws: years later, alan and i share a joyous moment

I **DIDN'T SEE** much of Alan after making the film in 1978. We would have seen each other more often had we lived on the same coast. But with Alan being in New York, and me in L.A., getting together for a cup of coffee is not that easy.

I next saw him in the late 1980s. He lived in Scarborough, about 30 miles north of New York City and a few miles south of Ossining, my hometown. He invited me up. I still smoked then, and Alan wouldn't allow any smoke in his house. So for dinner I sat outside on the patio and Alan and Barbara sat inside the house, but only a few feet away. We were separated by a screen door, but other than that it felt perfectly normal—three people very comfortably enjoying dinner together. Later, Alan and I drove around Ossining—I hadn't been home in years—and I was overwhelmed by the nostalgia of seeing my old neighborhood after such a long absence. I was pleased that Alan was there to share those moments with me.

Fast forward to 2002. I was in Vancouver shooting a two-hour TV movie and was worrying over the quality of the script—what else is new?—when the phone rang. I picked it up, but my mind was on the next day's scene.

PHONE VOICE
Peter, it's me, Alan. Congratulations.

PETER
Who?

ALAN
Alan, Alan Arkin.

PETER
Oh Alan—Hi.

ALAN
Congratulations.

PETER
I thought that's what you said.

ALAN
(*chuckling*)
I did.

PETER
For what?

ALAN

Your reviews.

PETER

Reviews??!

ALAN

Yeah—they're outstanding.

My mind searched for some show that could have just come out.

PETER

No kidding. You saw reviews?

ALAN

They loved you.

PETER

No kidding.

ALAN

Stop saying that. You sound busy.

PETER

Yeah—I'm up to my ass—

ALAN

So you haven't seen them.

PETER
What?

ALAN
The reviews, you moron.

PETER
What reviews are you talking about?

ALAN
(*laughing*)
The In-Laws.

PETER
The In-Laws??!

ALAN
Right.

PETER
(*confused*)
But that was ten years ago.

ALAN
The remake, moron.

PETER
(*finally understanding*)
Oh, the remake—it's out?

ALAN

(*chuckling*)

It's a turkey—the whole movie—in the toilet.

PETER

(*big grin*)

No kidding.

ALAN

(*now laughing*)

And you and I—we got raves—

better reviews for the remake than for the original.

PETER

(*full-out delight*)

No kidding. Better than the orig. . . .

(Can't finish—laughing too hard.)

wings of desire

THE PHONE RANG late one night. The call was from Germany. Of course I didn't know that at the time. I simply heard a man with a slight accent who spoke somewhat softly. He introduced himself but between a poor connection and a slight accent I didn't catch the name. That always makes me nervous. I'm uncomfortable speaking to someone who has properly introduced himself but instead of asking him to repeat his name, because I didn't catch it when the name was first said, I make believe I not only heard the name but I'm delighted to hear his voice as if it belongs to someone like Elvis Presley whom I never dreamed I'd get the opportunity to speak to.

At any rate . . . it appears that this man is calling regarding a script he's involved with—regarding a part he wants me to play. He speaks about John Cassavetes. I'm impressed with his words. He's not merely familiar with John; he's knowledgeable on a truly meaningful level.

When we talked about his script I'm impressed with his ease in admitting some uncertainty. Usually in these situations when someone wants you for something, everything is great—you're great, the part is great, the actors are great, he's great, everything's great—a car salesman. So I'm liking this man, but I'm still nervous, bothered by talking to someone whose name I don't know.

Then it comes to me from out of the blue. Not his name, but who he is. He's the German director who helmed *Paris, Texas*—a terrific movie. He's a world-class director, a man who makes singular movies, a man with an original voice. I'm now asking him specifics about my part—i.e., what does my character do, how does he make a living. Again his voice seems uncertain, seems to be searching for an answer. He says he's not sure, but he believes the character could be a number of things—a bricklayer, a salesman, a soldier. He's only sure of one thing. "What's that?" I ask. The character is an "ex-angel." Now, folks, I've heard of ex-wives, I've heard of ex-convicts, but I never heard of an ex-angel. I'm hooked. I'm ready to go. I said, "Tell me when to show up. I'll be there."

In Berlin I met Wim Wenders for the first time, in a bar. It was around midnight. He didn't have much time. He was probably still shooting. He knew where the plot was going, but there was no official script. He told me I'd be taken to wardrobe where I should pick out my costume. It felt like a Cassavetes movie.

At the wardrobe place, everything fell into place except for the hat. I tried on a bunch of them, but each hat had something about it that I didn't like.

We met Sunday in the hotel room to go over the costume. Wim was satisfied with all that we (the wardrobe girl and I) had chosen. Then we came to the problem with the hats. I put them on one at a time, pointing out what I didn't like. The brim on this one is too wide. This hat looks like I'm going to the opera and the one next to it like I'm going to a funeral. This brown one, the crown works full-face, but in profile it's no good, something missing, maybe the brim is too narrow. As for this hat, I suppose it would be good if I was playing Al Capone—and, oh, lay your eyes on this beauty—note the color—a bright purple!—for an ex-angel? I don't think so. Besides, tiny hats like this make your nose look big. So that's what we have, I tell him, that's it.

Wim is smiling. "I'll say this—maybe we don't have a hat, but we got a scene."

I'll be a monkey's uncle. Would you believe it?! That scene is in the picture.

I love Wim. He's wide open. He's not anxious, not fearful. If something tickles or interests him, he'll go for it. Similar to Cassavetes. Real loose. Very few like that.

In that connection, I should add a little something he admitted to me one day. He was talking about directing and he said:

WIM
You know when I first started directing and for many years
after I hated having to follow a script. I'd see some fantastic
location—some place so unique, that I had to tear myself
away. I wanted so badly to shoot it. The same for a sudden
fresh impulse for a new scene. A new approach that excited
me, compared to the familiar thing in the script. So I hated
scripts. They cramped me. They were like a jail. Now on this
picture I don't have a script. And every night before I go to
sleep I pray to God, "IF ONLY I HAD A SCRIPT."

I have to tell you one more story. We were shooting in Berlin. Now I've been everywhere and not just Paris, London, and Rome. I've been up and down the Adriatic, inside and out in Yugoslavia—in Marrakech,

Algeria—in the Russian Ukraine—Southern Japan. But at that time, this was the one city in the world with a wall that divided its population—people in West Berlin couldn't get to East Berlin, and vice versa.

I promised myself that on my first day off, I'd go to East Berlin to see what was on the other side of the wall. I was told that foreigners with a passport were allowed, but you couldn't bring much money. So my day off came, and I went to the checkpoint. It was like a frontier—plenty of guards with guns and a small building where you were questioned and filled out papers. I didn't like the atmosphere. The staff were sullen and stiff. Unfortunately, the form I had to fill out indicating I only had something like 10 dollars got wrinkled and spotted from their lousy pen. I tossed it down somewhat disdainfully in front of the inspector bureaucrat. He held it up by its tiny corner, dangling the form between his thumb and forefinger:

BUREAUCRAT

Das izz document. (pause) Das izz document. (now louder)

Das izz document.

He then summoned three huge guards and I was pushed forward and through a floor-to-ceiling curtain, ordered to undress, and body-searched, including my ass. They finished, then left, never saying a word.

I started dressing and was bending over to tie my shoes when one of the guards surreptitiously returned. Holding a finger to his lips, indicating I should be quiet, he turned and checked outside, peeping through a slit in the curtain. He then produced a piece of paper and a pen. "Please," he whispered, "your autograph."

What a moment. I grinned, pulled him toward me, and we hugged.

The story of *Wings of Desire* was often told through the unspoken interior thoughts of the characters—through what the character was thinking, as opposed to saying it to someone. The audience in the theater heard the words, but the other characters in the scene didn't hear them. On my last day, there was a little going-away party. They had brought some vodka—everyone toasted each other—hugs and kisses and as I headed down the corridor to the elevator, I heard my name called—"Peter—Peter, wait." It was Wim running after me: "I forgot the interior thoughts."

I didn't know what he was talking about. He never mentioned interior thoughts before. He then explained. "During a scene we might cut to you. Your mouth is closed. You're not speaking, but the audience will hear your voice and know that what they're hearing are your thoughts. So now I'd like to put you in a room with a live mike and let you talk. Say anything you want—anything at all that pops into your mind. Don't worry whether it's appropriate. You can think of your scenes if you want—see them in your mind's eye and say whatever." So that's what happened. They put me in a room and for a full two hours, I talked and they recorded. Wim was pleased, and I got on the plane. However that's not the end of the story.

It's six months later and I'm 15,000 feet above sea level in the Andes Mountains shooting a movie in a small Incan Indian village when I get a message to call Wim Wenders. It turns out that when I recorded my interior thoughts the sound was bad. Wim knew my current schedule and 10 days later, now in Los Angeles, I record my interior thoughts again—a second time. And that's what's in the film. And I liked them—liked what Wim did with them—thought they worked nicely.

Another indication of how Wim works . . . since I like to draw, I made quick sketches of people on the set. Wim picked up on that and used me drawing in a couple of scenes. I'd be talking to somebody or about somebody, and at the same time you'd see that I was drawing that person. Wim sees and hears everything. He's alert, quick, and flexible. He's terrific—one of a kind.

It never occurred to me that this picture would play in the United States I just assumed it would be seen in Europe. I was wrong, and thank the Lord for it. Stories about angels have a built-in magnetism. It not only played here, it was immensely successful. I can't tell you how many people were affected and delighted by it.

Just one more thing—a great deal of this movie was shot in Hitler's bunker. I didn't know we were going to shoot there and when I heard about it, I was only mildly interested. What could it be?—A place underground that was safe, protected from bombs? What a shock. It was huge beyond anything I ever imagined—deep enough for a 10-story building. Looking down from ground level to the bottom, the people below looked tiny. There were three or four levels and each level could accommodate about two football fields.

I don't know why I'm mentioning this except to say that for me, at least, it was a real eye opener. I guess der Fuehrer wanted some breathing room.

They call it a bomb shelter. Actually, it was a small-size city.

the princess bride

THE PRINCESS BRIDE was pure joy. Working on that movie wasn't working. It was just plain fun. The whole thing took three days, maybe two and a half. I flew to London, spent three days with Rob Reiner, and that great kid actor, Fred Savage, and that charming script, and the next day I was on a plane to Wim Wenders in Berlin for the sequel to *Wings of Desire.*

The big question on the first day of *The Princess Bride* was the makeup. The intention was to make me look older, more like a grandfather. The makeup people had a range of possibilities. They were thinking whitening my hair, bushing up my eyebrows, maybe eyeglasses, a moustache and/or beard, juicing up the bags under my eyes, etc., etc. They were all options and could be used in any number of combinations.

I didn't say anything. However, I must have looked ill, because that's the way I felt. And the more I heard about this makeup, the sicker I got. About then, Rob Reiner arrived. I don't know whether he noticed that I didn't look particularly delighted. I couldn't tell. The makeup people presented the various options, plus the various combinations of options, and added that whatever final choice Rob made, they could start immediately and comfortably finish by the end of the day. In fact, if Rob wanted to see two different versions before making his final decision, they could swing that.

It was up to Rob to make the choices so they could get started. Everybody felt that Rob would need a little time so they weren't surprised at the pause he took before answering. It wasn't long. "NO MAKEUP. HE LOOKS FINE." That's all he said, and he left.

Well, folks, I had an ear-to-ear grin. I was so happy, so tickled with Rob—what he said and the way he said it—it was the perfect beginning, and from there on everything got even more perfect.

The next day we started shooting. First shot I enter my grandson's bedroom. He's not feeling well. I say a few lines and cut. Rob likes the first take; he prints it. He likes the second take; he prints it. Before the third take, he comes on the set and says, "Peter, after your second line, how about this gesture?" He demonstrates the gesture. I love it. We do a third take. The gesture works like a charm. We're finished and on to the next scene.

I have been doing TV and film for almost fifty years, and that was the first time in all those years that any director actually demonstrated, actually acted out a gesture for me to copy, and thank God for that. I can imagine how I would have reacted—withering contempt comes to mind—it's simply unimaginable that any director would be such an assbucket. But here's the difference: Rob is an actor—a terrific actor—and the gesture was a kick for me to watch and fun for me to do. I confess I have a soft spot in my heart for directors who are also actors.

However, I can't complete this chapter without recounting a "FIRST," something that never happened to me before and will never happen to

Fred Savage and Peter

me again. For me *The Princess Bride* was a movie without a blemish, perfect for both kids and adults. However, when the movie was completed there was one thing wrong—one glaring thing—one major defect. The last line in the movie. It's my line to my grandson, "As you like it." The sound was so bad, it killed the line. It killed the movie's ending. I knew nothing about this. For me, the picture was completed. Yet six months later, I'm in a play at the Ahmanson Theatre, it's Saturday, it's that time between the end of the matinee performance and the curtain going up for the evening show. It's also the time that Rob arrives at the theater with a camera guy and a couple of lights. They come get me from the dressing room and the three of us roam around backstage. We're in a wide corridor and someone says this looks good. In no time we're ready to shoot. I take one step then turn and face the lens. I'm talking to an imaginary grandson who's in his bed. I say the last line of the movie, "As you like it." We do one take and Rob yells: "Great, that's it, we're finished." He shakes my hand and leaves. When you, the reader, see the film in the theater, you'll see that last line—the one that was shot after the Saturday matinee backstage at the Ahmanson Theatre, and I might add it's a great reading. Rob meant what he said—a bull's-eye—I hit it out of the park, first take.

happy new year

IN THIS MOVIE I had to play three characters:

1. A 40-year-old sophisticated jewel thief;

2. A 75-year-old millionaire living in posh Palm Beach, Florida, his mind just beginning to show the wear and tear of old age; and

3. His 68-year-old sister. A woman totally together who looks out for her brother's well-being.

I'm a sophisticated, experienced, and successful con man/jewel thief. Charley Durning is my friend and sidekick. We've worked together for years. We're a great team. On this caper, I will impersonate a 75-year-old millionaire, and Charley will impersonate the millionaire's chauffeur.

The movie was based on a French film of the same name. Written and directed by Claude Lelouch (*A Man and a Woman*) with Lino Ventura and Françoise Fabian—I loved that picture with all my heart—a great love story woven into a great jewelry-store caper.

What made the robbery—the actual stickup with guns—so compelling was the brilliant con executed prior to the robbery. Two thieves, myself and Charley Durning, pull their Rolls Royce up in front of a posh jewelry store in Palm Beach, Florida. They enter the shop, and the con begins. I'm 75 years old and it's difficult to walk, but with my chauffeur's help I manage the steps. Looking old and distraught, I approach the jewelry-store owner. I explain I'm worried about my wife. She's in the hospital—it's very serious, and she might not make it. I want to cheer her up with a piece of jewelry—something extraordinary, whatever the cost. The price is not a consideration. But I know nothing about jewelry, and unfortunately whatever I pick out turns out to be the least expensive item. So I'll have to rely on the owner's judgment. He nods sympathetically. "I'll do everything I can."

The con, as it develops, requires another character, and a week or so later she arrives at the jewelry store—the old guy's sister (me in drag). The sister somewhat emotionally approaches the store owner and wants to enlist his cooperation. At all costs, she doesn't want her brother's feelings hurt. He must never know that his sick wife dislikes the jewelry that he bought for her. The sister returns it and picks out something else. Something even more expensive. The owner understands; mum's the word.

The owner is now beautifully positioned for the actual heist. The mere sight of either the brother or the sister and he's beaming, his eyes dancing at the sight of money, his arms open wide in a gesture of warm welcome.

Now the love story. The female owner of the antique shop next door to the jewelry store is awesome—knockout gorgeous with a sense of humor and great legs. She has no idea that the old man who engages her in conversation regarding the antique chair in her store window is actually a 40-year-old jewel thief who can't take his eyes off her. He's smitten—wants her bad.

I can't tell you the whole story of the movie. It's on tape. It's not easy to find, but I recommend it. I should mention that in the Lelouch film, there was no sister. There was just the old man and the chauffeur. However, for this movie the studio wanted more—I don't know what to name it—let's call it ZIP. I didn't feel the movie needed more zip, but it got me—thinking would be too strong a word—let's say the "zip" word would occasionally cross my mind.

It must have been there the night I was having dinner with Elaine May and talking about my mother. At one point, Elaine interrupted me and asked me to repeat what I just said. I asked why? She said, "Do it." I did. She said, "You do a good impression of your mother. You should do it in some movie." It struck me how much fun that would be!! What a kick! What fun, and mother would love it. From there it's only half a step to *How about this movie*? How could I do it in this movie, and from there it's not a big leap to the old guy has a sister and she sounds and acts like my mother.

So it wasn't the sister idea that got me, it was playing mother—and I could write my mother's part with my eyes shut—and I could write it fast, in the time it takes you to put this book down.

MEET PETER FALK, PETER FALK, AND PETER FALK.

★★★.
Don't Miss It."
—Chris Chase,
NEW YORK DAILY NEWS

"★★★."
Charming."
—Jami Bernard,
NEW YORK POST

"★★★."
—Joseph Gelmis,
NEW YORK NEWSDAY

Prebook Date: October 19
Street Date: November 12

HAPPY NEW YEAR

**A multi-faceted comedy
about a gem of a jewel heist.**

Suggested Retail
Price: $79.95

COLUMBIA PICTURES PRESENTS "HAPPY NEW YEAR" CHARLES DURNING
A JERRY WEINTRAUB PRODUCTION PETER FALK MUSIC BY BILL CONTI EXECUTIVE PRODUCER ALLAN RUBAN PRODUCTION DESIGNER WILLIAM J. CASSIDY
TOM COURTENAY WENDY HUGHES SCREENPLAY BY WARREN LANE PRODUCED BY JERRY WEINTRAUB DIRECTED BY JOHN G. AVILDSEN
DIRECTOR OF PHOTOGRAPHY JAMES CRABE, A.S.C.

RCA
Columbia Pictures
HOME VIDEO

Beta VHS
hi-fi hi-fi

Let's talk about makeup for this movie. Let's talk about three hours in the makeup chair every morning—actually almost 3 1/2 for the woman. Let's talk about the foam rubber mask pasted to my face—a mask that couldn't come off for the next 12 hours. Let's talk about Fort Lauderdale, Florida, in the middle of August. The blistering heat, from 98 to 103 degrees, and the humidity you couldn't breathe even if your face was bare. How about my face under that foam rubber, under the paste, the stickum, whatever the hell you call it—under that wig for 12 hours in that suffocating heat. It's a good thing I was the producer, because if it had been anybody else, he would've been gone, strangled to death by the beginning of August.

The actual truth is, as opposed to my ranting, I so enjoyed playing my mother that when I was actually acting I forgot all that crap on my face. I was, as they say today, "Doing it, dude"—having a ball.

If you get a chance, see the picture. It's worth a look. I want you to see me playing my mother.

A **BOOK CAME** out in the '90s titled *Roommates*. A few years later based on that book we made the movie *Roommates*. Who were these roommates? One was a typical 19-year-old American male starting his freshman year at college. The other was his unemployed 90-year-old grandfather. You read it right. He was 90 years old. He went to some classes but he was essentially looking for a job. His real name is unpronounceable but for, who knows, maybe 70 years the guys he worked with called him Rocky. Why, I don't know. He was tiny—5 foot tall, 110 pounds. But he was fiery. He was one of my favorite characters. Columbo of course was my number one most favorite, but Rocky was right there high on the list. He was extraordinary and I was crazy about him.

When I think of Rocky I think of a man who came to this country from Lithuania at the turn of the century (1901) and immediately started working 16 hours a day, went to night school, became a master baker, and spent his whole life, hear this, going to bed at 9:30 and getting up at 4:00 in the morning.

When I think of Rocky, I think of a man who at 85 years of age was forced to retire and it was his union that did the forcing. They had rules regarding a worker's age. So what did he do? He moonlighted! He snuck around and, without the union knowing, worked various jobs. And even sneaking around, he still put in 30 hours a week. How did he describe it? A vacation. To him, if you're alive, you work. If you're alive and don't work, you're dead. It's that simple.

There's a scene in the movie where Rocky is in the hospital. He's just had a very serious operation. The ether is just wearing off. His eyelids start to flutter. His mouth is moving and he's making sounds. Standing next to the bed is his grandson, Max, and the doctor. Max lifts Rocky's hand and gently rubs his fingers.

MAX

Everything went good, Pop. You feel all right?
(Rocky, very weak, semiconscious, nods his head. He's okay.)

MAX

Good—anything you want. Cool drink, lemonade—
whatever—I'll get it.

Rocky mumbles something. It's difficult to understand. Actually it's unintelligible.

Max leans in. Puts his face very close to Rocky's. Their heads are practically touching. Max loves his grandfather. He is profoundly relieved that the crisis is over. He whispers into Rocky's ear asking him to repeat what it is that he wants.

Rocky's eyes open. He moves his hand upward and touches Max's

courtesy of Photofest

D.B. Sweeney and Peter

face, pulling the ear closer to his mouth. Rocky whispers something that brings a smile to Max's face.

MAX

I'll get it for you. You'll have it in 20 minutes.

As Max straightens up and releases Rocky's hand, the doctor asks him what is it that Rocky wanted.

MAX

I shoulda known. He wants the classified section of the newspaper. Wants to see if there are any job openings.

I could go on and on about Rocky, but you get the picture. They threw away the mold when they made him. However, there is one major aspect of this production that I must talk about.

I've been doing this acting thing for a long time, and in all my years I never felt what I felt about *Roommates.* I was convinced that this movie was one scene away from being a money maker. And we had that scene. It was written. And I wrote it. And the director loved it. And the producers loved it. And they had found a terrific location for it. AND IT WAS NEVER SHOT. The scene was put on the schedule. But it was *never shot.* The head of Disney back in Hollywood vetoed the scene and ordered the director to shoot the original scene that was in the script.

Here is the scene that was never shot. It's been read by only seven people. You taste it. See what you think. Imagine it coming immediately after the scene in the hospital room where Rocky, still emerging from the ether, only semiconscious, asks for the classified section. The scene starts as follows:

It's very early in the morning. Rocky enters a delicatessen. It's a very small shop. True, it has a glass counter with cold cuts and a couple of shelves with canned food, but it's not where'd you would go to shop. More like a corner store. But above the door at the end of the counter is a big sign, RESTAURANT.

Rocky is puzzled when he goes through the door. The room is bare— no sign of a restaurant. There is a carved wooden counter. In its day, it could have been a bar, and behind it is the biggest fireplace in the city of Pittsburgh.

I'm describing this place because it's odd. It has atmosphere. You're interested in the setting but puzzled by it. You sense some faded grandeur. Rocky of course is uncertain—looking around not sure where to go next. He's holding a brown paper bag. He holds it chest-high and it sits horizontally in the palms of both his hands.

A man in a white apron and a chef's hat arrives.

CHEF
You want something, mister?

(Rocky is annoyed by the tone of his voice, takes his time
answering—finally:)

ROCKY
You say something?

CHEF
You heard me—answer me.

ROCKY
I'm going to answer you, sir, but allow me to note that I'm in
my nineties, and more than anything I'd like to be in my
eighties—so I could walk over there and knock you on your
fat, ugly ass—

The Chef can't help himself, can't entirely conceal the beginning of
a smile. This old geezer is a real character.

CHEF
May I ask, is the boss expecting you?

ROCKY
Yes, he is. Bubba John set it up.

CHEF
You know Bubba John?

ROCKY
For 63 years. Bubba told me the restaurant is in the market
for a baker—I'm a baker. He said I should meet his boss.
He set it up.

just one more thing   277

CHEF

I see. Okay. Well, the boss is upstairs in the restaurant
working on the books.

ROCKY

Well, tell him I'm here. I got something for him.
You want to see it?

Rocky places his package down on the wooden counter. He carefully
reaches into the brown paper bag and removes a glorious six-layered
chocolate cake. The Chef is naturally surprised but visibly impressed.
This is the work of a master baker. This is a world-class cake. Rocky has
removed a separate small piece, which he offers the Chef. The man's
face says it all. This is as good as it gets.

The Chef with the cake heads up the stairs to the restaurant to get
the boss.

ROCKY

(calling to the Chef)
Make him taste it.

CHEF

Right.

ROCKY

Not just look at—it's got to go into the mouth.

CHEF

Right.

ROCKY

I mean it—if you can't do it, I will. I want it in his mouth.

Upstairs in the restaurant, the boss is preoccupied. Surrounded by paper, bank statements, financial records. He's making notes. He's not interested, at 7:30 in the morning, in seeing people who are looking for a job.

CHEF

(*to the boss*)

He baked a cake and he wants you to taste it.

BOSS

(*head down; making notes; doesn't look up*)

Wants me to do what?!!

CHEF

Taste his cake.

BOSS

(*still writing*)

A nut case, right?

CHEF

Wrong. Take a second. I promise on my mother's eyes you'll be knocked out.

The Boss is irritated, but he'll take a second. He puts out his hand, receives a tiny cube of cake. He's chewing and when the taste hits his tongue his head bobs approvingly up and down as he extends his hand for a second piece.

BOSS

I want this guy. He's great. Where is he?

The Boss and his Chef head through the restaurant to the top of the stairs. By now, the Boss is working on his third taste of cake. They reach the top of the stairs. The Chef stops. So does the Boss. The Chef points downward to Rocky, who's leaning on the carved wooden counter.

Rocky, alone with his thoughts, is unaware of the two men watching him from above. The Boss is staring, studying the man who baked that glorious cake. Finally:

BOSS

He's too old. Forget it.

He turns and heads back to his office. We cut outside.

There are light snowflakes starting to fall. The door opens and Rocky emerges. He's carrying his brown paper bag, the cake inside. He looks grim and as he moves forward toward the camera—as his face grows into a closeup—he looks even grimmer. We stay on him as he passes us and starts to recede. We see him, now full-figure, stop at a park bench. We watch as he places his cake next to a homeless guy stretched out asleep on his public bed, his head nestled in the crook of his elbow.

The scene that was shot, the original one that was in the script, had me and another old man sitting on a bench and making remarks about two women that were walking by.

It was a nothing scene. It had no power—but, as they say, you can't win them all.

epilogue

MY AGENT CALLED the other day with an offer for a part in a new film. As always, my first question: "How much are they paying?" Some things never change. We can all say that about our lives, and there's some truth in it—some things never change It's certainly true in my case—but with one EXCEPTION. And that EXCEPTION just happened. I've just WRITTEN A BOOK! Talk about change! Who would dream I would ever write a book! Not me! Not my wife, not my doctor, dogs, family, friends, or acquaintances. Let me sum up by saying it was a blast! The funny stuff. Reliving it. Putting it on paper. If you had as much fun reading it as I had writing it, you'll be dancing on the ceiling. For those of you still in your chairs, I'm delighted you're still awake. I love you for staying with me until the end.